640.41 Red

Red wine on the carpet.

PRICE: $24.95 (3559/ba   )

RED WINE
ON THE CARPET

RED WINE
ON THE CARPET

Secret tips from
COUNTRY LIFE'S
Housekeeper, Mrs DANVERS

SWAN·HILL
PRESS

Publisher's Note

Every effort has been made to update and check the
information in this book but in a few instances changes may
have occurred between time of proofs and publication.

Copyright © 2007 IPC Media Limited 2007
© Matthew Rice (illustrations)

First published in the UK in 2007
by Swan Hill Press, an imprint of Quiller Publishing Ltd

British Library Cataloguing-in-Publication Data
A catalogue record for this book
is available from the British Library

ISBN 978 1 84689 015 4

Illustrations by Matthew Rice

Design and typesetting by Paul Saunders
Printed in Great Britain by St Edmundsbury Press Ltd.,
Bury St Edmunds, Suffolk.

Swan Hill Press

An imprint of Quiller Publishing Ltd
Wykey House, Wykey, Shrewsbury, SY4 1JA
Tel: 01939 261616 Fax: 01939 261606
E-mail: info@quillerbooks.com
Website: www.countrybooksdirect.com

Contents

GARDENS & OUTDOORS

CHRISTMAS

PETS & WILDLIFE

PARTIES

FOOD & DRINK

Foreword

Thank heavens for Mrs Danvers, the world's most famous housekeeper. Toss her a problem and she will smoothly deliver the answer. Whether you need to know how to remove red wine from a carpet (use blotting paper – never salt, white wine or soda) or how to clean stuffed animals (use a hairdryer on cold), or if you'd like to master the fine art of dusting (it's all in the brushes), she will have the solution for you in the blink of an eye. She will have undertaken many of the tasks herself at some stage in her long career, and if not, her great network of contacts ensures that the correct approach to any problem will be available.

It is fitting that this volume should appear in the centenary of the birth of Daphne du Maurier, who celebrated the original Mrs Danvers in *Rebecca* (published in 1938), the ever-vigilant housekeeper at Manderley. Happily for the *Country Life* office, the current Mrs Danvers doesn't glide quite so silently as Judith Anderson in Hitchcock's film adaptation – although she does have an alarming tendency to pop up when you least expect her.

The current grande dame of housekeepers follows in the great tradition of Hannah Glasse and Mrs Beeton, and is as essential for reading today as those two greats were in their time. She is a formidably practical lady. When her first column appeared in *Country Life* on April 1, 2004, she was asked whether she minded starting on April Fool's Day. She replied: 'Mr Editor, I don't believe in nonsense and hokum. If you are worried about that sort of thing, I am not the right person to write for you.' Quite so. Her knowledge is extraordinary, ranging from using geese as watch-dogs and making everything around the home sparkle to building an ornamental clock tower and having a flag made to fly from it. Nobody reading this book will fail to discover some vital way of improving his or her home or lifestyle. Many of her replies to some quite eccentric inquiries put to her by the readers of *Country Life* verge on bluntness. She has little time for slackers, and you should not, as one reader discovered, seek to kill a wasp.

Her answers have fixed broken crockery, soothed ailments and, in a few cases, saved marriages. This is unquestionably a valuable book and a great tonic to this vulgar age.

MARK HEDGES
Editor-in-Chief, *Country Life*

Removing Red Wine Stains from the Carpet

I am unusually clumsy, especially, I confess, after a glass or two of red wine. Hence, my carpet is nastily stained with old wine to an extent that I am now thoroughly ashamed of it. I have considered moving house or buying a claret-coloured carpet, but what can I do that would be easier?

I never throw red wine on my carpet, but I have taken advice from experts and they tell me that, with recently spilt red, you should first blot it up with dry blotting paper or a J-cloth, then attack it with a good carpet shampoo. Do not use salt, white wine or soda, because these are likely to make things worse.

For old stains, try putting a solution of equal parts of glycerine and water on the spots for an hour, then sponge off with water. An alternative (if your carpet is small enough) is to do nothing to the stains, but to take the carpet to a dry cleaner, explaining what the stain is. They prefer to tackle the job without any outside interference by bungling amateurs.

Cleaning Decanters

I have inherited some decanters from an unhygienic elderly relative who seems so have used them to store oxtail and mulligatawny soup. How do I clean them up?

∽

If there is a good reason for making decanters in shapes impossible to clean – helping the wine to breathe? Helping the butler to take a nip? – I do not know it. There are as many solutions to dirty decanters as there are people who need them. If the decanter is encrusted with old soup on the inside, you will probably need something gritty to swirl round the glass to break off the encrustations. Traditionally, lead shot was used, and tiny copper balls are on sale at Peter Jones (of course). But I would recommend fine sand from the builders' merchant (or sandpit). Add washing-up liquid and warm water (never hot, the glass might break) and swirl.

If your decanter is merely cloudy, other professionals have advised me to tackle the problem with a heaped table-spoon of dentifrice dissolved in half a tumbler of warm water, or stinging nettles plunged down into a decanter filled with water. Clever though these recipes are, my solution would be first to glug a few spoonfuls of thick house-hold bleach into the decanter (although a purist would shudder at the idea), swirl it round and leave for a couple of hours. If you do not want to poison your guests, make sure every last trace has been washed out before using.

I would try this first and only fiddle about with shot, nettles and the like as a final resort. To dry a decanter, mop out with rolled kitchen paper and leave overnight close to the Aga or a radiator, on a wooden drying rack, if you can find one.

Dear Mrs Danvers, might I add a postscript to your advice about cleaning cloudy decanters? I suggest your correspondent takes (or sends) the Waterford to Mr Basil Loveridge, Unit 1, Avonbury Court, Brackley, Northamptonshire (01993 706490). He did a splendid job last year in restoring the sparkle to five of our decanters which had become 'milky' and which had resisted all my attempts to get them clean.

Yours sincerely,
NIGEL C. HOLLINGDALE

Dear Mrs Danvers, I have just read your column about cleaning cloudy decanters, in Country Life, *and was rather concerned with some of the advice it offered. Telling members of the public to use hot water in a crystal decanter is, I feel, questionable, as almost every single cracked decanter, bowl or vase that we see (and, over the years, there have been thousands) has been caused by the use of hot water.*

We can remove the stains from decanters, but, as you point out, it is costly. Prices start at about £40, plus postage and packing.

There are many other repairs we can do – for example, taking the chips out of a wineglass or tumbler will cost £11.75, including VAT – less if we are repairing a large quantity.

As for superglue (and I know you did not recommend anyone to use it), when it comes to minor repairs, there is a product widely available to the public, made by Loctite, called Glass Bond. This is very similar to the industrial versions we use under ultraviolet lighting. The average person can glue simple breaks back together and leave the glass in sunlight to cure. Superglue is only suitable for sticking fingers together.

I am the third generation of Wilkinsons to run the family business in South-East London – my 20-year-old daughter, Jodie, who joined the business this year, will, I hope, be the next. We have held the Royal Warrant to The Queen as glass restorers since 1985.

Yours sincerely,
DAVID WILKINSON

Polishing Furniture

The staff do not seem to be able to get a good shine on our antique furniture. Are they simply lazy or am I buying the wrong kind of polish?

～

Well, you will have to sort our your own staff, I'm afraid, but here are some observations on furniture polish, so you can see where you are going wrong (but take advice before embarking on anything major). I have spoken to a top antiques restorer to get this information and allied it with our own experience.

Polishing furniture is not as simple as it appears. For a start, which wax you use depends on the state of the wood. Furniture restorers often have to strip old wood of various accretions such as French polish, if it is not appropriate, and this means starting a new polished surface from scratch. West Dean College, which teaches restoration, uses a recipe from veteran restorer Stanley Block, but do not try this at home without expert advice. Raw carnauba wax (from a Brazilian palm) is melted and dissolved in pure turpentine and allowed to cool to a firm consistency. It gives an unbeatable finish, but is extremely hard work to apply.

An alternative is to mix pure beeswax with pure turpentine, again to a workable consistency. This is also hard work and the polish tends to get more solid as the turps evaporates (you can remelt and add more, in this case).

Once the patina is good, then it needs simply to be maintained. It is important here to avoid any polish with silicone or cellulose in the ingredients, but any good beeswax-based polish, used twice a year, should do the trick. Dust and burnish the furniture weekly. We prefer Antiquax, because it is easy to apply and comes in a sensible, wide-brimmed tin which makes it easy to insert a duster. Polishes in narrow-topped jars may be just as good- but they are harder to reach.

The Best Furniture Polish

I have some fine antique furniture in walnut, mahogany and oak. What sort of polish do you recommend?

Purists make their own from a mixture of beeswax and turpentine (artists' turpentine, not white spirit). You should melt the beeswax in a tin in a cool oven and add the same amount of turpentine. Let both melt, and then mix them together. Pour into a polish tin which is wide and shallow so you can get a duster in easily. If, when set, the consistency is too hard (it should be quite firm), melt it again and add a bit more turpentine. I would suggest you use this a few times on furniture that has had little polish over the years to get the patina back. After that, an ordinary furniture polish of beeswax will do, but make sure that it is intended for antiques and doesn't contain silicone which can be damaging.

How to Dust

Due to unforeseen circumstances, I shall have to dust the house, which I have not done before. Can you give me any hints?

～

Dusting is a fine art and, like painting, it is essential to have the right brushes. Depending on the depth of your pocket, you will need six or seven, each for a special purpose. First, you must have one of ostrich feathers from Italy, with a long handle (at £5 not so expensive, now that we farm the birds in Europe).

Contrary to the evidence of silent films, they do not knock Ming vases off pedestals, but do a fine job of wafting dust off shelves-full of precious antiques. Next, for your library, you should invest in a goat-hair library brush (£7), rather like a giant pastry brush, but with soft hair rather than bristles. With this you can lovingly stroke the tops of gold-edged pages and Morocco-bound spines. For cobwebs (and who is immune from them?), there is a special long-handled Westphalian cobweb brush (£14). This is of tough horsehair and shaped like a mushroom. The best versions can be tilted at an angle. A goat-hair version (£14), for softer work, is also available.

Of course, you cannot do without ordinary hand brushes – these should be in horsehair (£5.50) for difficult corners and goat hair (£9.50) just because it is so lovely to stroke – although it is ideal for dining tables and other polished tops. And, for the cleaner who has everything, there is even a computer cleaning brush (£13) from Sweden, with pig bristles on one side for the keyboard and goat hair on the other for the sensitive bits. This one would also do for cleaning banisters.

They all come from Manufactum mail order (0800 096 0937) and can be transported from room to room in a multi-pocketed apron. The Chelsea Gardener (020 7352 5656) does a good one (from £29.95). Note: you do not need a single yellow duster to discolour everything in the weekly wash.

Bathroom Panels

I have bought a house which has a pleasant, large bath-room with a large Georgian sash window and a central, freestanding bath. But it has been panelled up to dado height with undistinguishable, even clumsy, panels. I would like to dress these up a bit but, after the cost of moving, I am keen to do it on the cheap.

～

Bathrooms are not intended to be great architectural statements, but areas for privacy and comfort. You must, therefore, keep any grandiose ideas of linenfold carving of bolection moulding under severe control. It sounds as though your bathroom was panelled by the local carpenter or even a do-it-yourself character but, strangely, this is to your advantage as informal, even bodged work can be given bags of charm.

The first impression you want to make is that this is 17th or 18th-century work rather than 1983, so you should dis-tress the panels with a chain, such as the dog lead. Then you should devise subterfuge dowels which instantly give an ageing effect. This is easy: before painting the panelling, push normal drawing pins in pairs into the top and bottom of the uprights between each recessed panel. If in doubt, just imagine where the dowels would be needed to hold the whole together.

Now paint the panels in two different shades of the same colour. Farrow & Ball's dead flat oil is a good choice – never use gloss on panelling, it is quite beastly. I would pick a pair of soft greys, possibly Hardwick White and Pigeon, or beiges such as String or String and Fawn. The lighter colour should be used for the panels themselves and the darker for the surrounding frames, especially the drawing pins, and the rest of the wood work – doors, skirting, window surrounds, etc.

The walls above the dado and the ceiling should be even lighter – Farrow & Ball's off-white Pointing, for example, which is pleasantly warm and creamy (and, thankfully, nothing like magnolia).

Finally, a touch of wax polish on the panelled areas gives a good antique effect and adds a nice depth of colour. Use a normal high-quality furniture wax and concentrate on giving the curves and mouldings the most shine. You will probably only need to do this once.

Moth-Proofing

What shall I do about clothes moths? They have eaten my favourite cashmere scarf and have completely demolished two old Victorian tartan shawls. In the old days, I filled my drawers and cupboards with Vapona moth killer, which worked. But this has now been withdrawn from sale because of health scares (to humans, not moths). I am at my wit's end.

~

Since moth killers have been withdrawn because of organphosphorus, there has been an explosion of the winged pests and cashmere-loving caterpillars. Moths are attracted to all forms of natural-fibres (except cotton) such as wool, alpaca, silk and camelhair and especially like clothes that have not been cleaned properly.

The problem is that the withdrawn products were killers and, in closed cupboards, would slay both moths and caterpillars. What is left on the market are moth preventatives – products which smell unpleasant to the nasty things and therefore, should manage to deter them. The problem with traditional mothballs, which work like this, is that they smell awful to humans too.

There are now alternatives on the market in the form of cubes of camphor, which smell pretty awful as well, to a French anti-moth proofer I bought at the local hardware store. It contains dichlorobenzene and sounds pretty unsafe for both children and animals since the warnings on the packet are pretty ferocious. More appealing are Colibri sachets which smell quite pleasant to me but, apparently, not to moths. Finally Rita Konig (*Domestic Bliss*, Ebury) says that conkers in drawers seem, magically, to do the trick. Since this is a good time of year to collect a few, why not try piling them round clothes made of natural fabrics (moths are not interested in Polyester or even Crimplene)?

It will, of course, not help with already-laid eggs and already-doomed cashmere sweaters, so I'm afraid you are in for a war of attrition with many tragedies yet to come.

Please take care only to swat clothes moths – the tiny beige ones. Others such as the hummingbird hawk moth and the yellow underwing are not only harmless but also increasingly rare.

Lavender as a Moth Proof

One of the great luxuries in life, in my view, is lavender-scented bedlinen and lavender bags in the wardrobe. Have you any source or supply? And will the scent deter moths?

～

My moth expert, Gadon Robinson, is uncertain about the efficacy of lavender bags, although that and other herbals, such as cloves, vetiver and sandalwood, may help. Anyway, the scent of lavender in clothes and sheets is, as you say, a great luxury in its own right.

My own source of lavender bags, linen scent and lavender water is Long Barn (01962 777873). To stop moths, Richard Norris, a partner in the firm which grows acres of lavender on a farm near Winchester, recommends that, when you pack away your winter clothes (any minute now, with luck), you should freeze them for up to 10 days, then pack them away in airtight plastic with a lavender bag inside.

An alternative is to buy his lavendin (*Lavandula intermedia*) essential oil (£4 for 10ml). 'This is much more robust than lavender [*Lavandula angustifolia*, £5 for 10ml]. It seems a shame to waste aromatherapy-grade oil on the little critters.' Pour this onto strips of card and leave these in the wardrobe.

However, leaving the moth problem aside, we use Long Barn's Linen Water (£10 a litre) in the steam iron and squirt their pillow spray (£15 for 200ml) onto the bed at night, as the scent is thought to help you sleep.

Their mini lavender bags (£1 each) are ideal to put in clothes drawers or you can make your own from a 200g bag of loose lavender (£4.50). Mr Norris adds that the present of a bag of lavender is always welcome, especially for people ill in bed or in hospital.

Making Lavender Bags

I have lots of lavender hedges in my garden, which my gardener has cut back, removing all the seed heads. These are sitting in a box in my house and I would like to harvest them to make into lavender bags. Do you have a method which doesn't leave dust and leaves everywhere?

Yes, take a large pillowcase and put the lavender into it. Scuffle it about inside the case until the seeds have been detached from the stalks. Remove the stalks and put them on the compost. What is left inside the pillowcase will be ready for lavender bags. A nice idea is to fill good-looking bowls with what you have left – they will scent a room.

Dyeing Clothes

My dry cleaner has stopped dyeing clothes, so I shall have to do it myself. I have a favourite black cotton jacket which has gone grey and dull with repeated washings. How can I spruce it up?

～

You have picked the perfect combination for home dyeing. First, your jacket is cotton and, I assume, can be washed in a machine. Next, you are not trying to change its colour but to improve what is already there. Changing colour, even from light to dark, is fraught with problems. First, if you try to dye yellow into blue, it goes green and, obviously enough, you cannot dye from dark to light.

More complex include differences between synthetic and natural fibres. For instance, the thread used for stitching a cotton jacket together may be synthetic and not take up the dye (I have seen an extremely chic, vintage Yves St Laurent safari jacket dyed black with its stitching still in the original beige.)

Next, we have found that the cold-water dyes needed for more sensitive fabrics than linen or cotton are not so effective. They are also enormously messy, involving plastic buckets, tongs and rubber gloves. I was initially nervous of machine wash dyes (Dylon is the leading brand) because I refused to believe that large quantities of hot, black dye swashing round in the drum could ever be rinsed away. But they were. You will need, as well as the dye recommended on the packet (we used two packets for two jackets and a pair of trousers), 500g of salt. Curiously, the amount of salt stays the same however much dye is needed.

All this is dropped on top of the clothes in the drum and put in as hot a wash as the fabric will take. You will need to pre-wash the clothes and put on a hot wash programme after the dyeing is done to clear any residue, so it is worth having plenty to dye in one batch.

Our sample worked perfectly on all three garments and, since we were simply renewing the black, we could proba-bly have reduced the amount of dye – but it is not expen-sive and we stuck to the instructions rigidly. Unlike many instructions, we found Dylon's to be clear and helpful – and, what is more, they worked.

The Perfect Log Fire

Neither my wife nor I seem able to light our log fire. It either never gets started or, if we turn our backs, goes out. We live in the country and have plenty of kindling and logs, but I am thinking of giving the wretched thing up and putting in coal and gas.

～

You must do no such thing. Coal and gas fires are just about acceptable in a first-floor London drawing room (coal is so difficult to store and carry upstairs), but are an outrage in a country house. Your kindling and logs – are they the right ones, and are they properly seasoned? Only ash logs will burn from green wood – all the rest need several months in a wood shed before they dry out enough to burn. No soft wood is suitable because it flares and explodes into showers of sparks which could set your house alight. Soft wood is a false economy.

But, supposing you have a good supply of dry hardwood and some dry, seasoned kindling (bits of plywood, wood off-cuts and fallen twigs can all be used) you will also need a supply of firelighters. We prefer the ones which come packed in silver foil so that they do not cover your hands with smelly bits of stuff impregnated with paraffin. One firelighter should be enough for an average fire and you will not need any crumpled newspapers in this case. Set it at the bottom of the grate or, if the fire is an open one, on top of the accumulated wood ash.

On top of this, erect a pyramid of small sticks and other kindling. Set light to the firelighter and wait a moment until the kindling has well and truly caught. At this point, lay on some smallish logs and let them catch fire before you pile on larger ones. You will find that success comes from getting a good core burning with small, easily burned logs before piling on tree branches and so on. Just like a bonfire, once the core is glowing hot, you can get away with anything – you will even find that a few twigs laid on at breakfast time the next morning will catch again.

Cleaning Steel Fenders

I have two very handsome steel fenders but over the damp winter they have become rusty. Can you tell me how to clean them up – and how to stop rust returning?

~

Here we have only brass fenders, which are much easier to care for, so, having been most impressed with the brightly shining steel fenders at the Georgian House in Charlotte Square, Edinburgh, which belongs to the National Trust for Scotland, I asked its most helpful curator, Ian Gow, and his colleagues just how they did it.

First, Mr Gow told me that, in general, the Trust's view elsewhere is not to have its steel shiny but, in Charlotte Square, the policy is to let fenders look just as they would have done when first bought in the 18th century. At the time they would have gleamed like silver. He then put me in touch with Rodney French, whose long-established Edinburgh firm, Lonsdale & Dutch (23b Howe Street), deals with such things.

Mr French says he cleans rusted steel to a good, bright shine with his polishing machine using mops and sateen carborundum sandpaper. This takes off all the rust. Lesser mortals, he says, could use a wet and dry sandpaper by hand. A light coating of rust might even come away with a rubbing of fine wire wool or a Scotchbrite scourer, normally used for scrambled-egg encrusted pans.

Then, he says, a polish with Brasso wadding should give a good finish. Moira Gibson, housekeeper at the Georgian

House, says she maintains the polish by giving the fenders a dose of Solvol Autosol (to be found at car accessory shops). 'I spread it on with balls of cotton wool, all in one direction, leave two minutes and then buff it off with a soft, clean cloth. I do this about once a year and the coating helps protect the steel. I also buff the steel regularly without Autosol. If there is any rust, I take it out with fine wire wool – grade 000 or 0000 – and then give it a coating of Autosol.' So you see, steel fenders are not as easy as brass. In the 18th century, of course, a house such as that in Charlotte Square would have had several 'tweenies' and housemaids to do the work for you.

Laundry – Keeping Linen Soft

Please can you tell me how to keep my linen soft. I have tried every fabric conditioner on the market but, apart from providing some strange smells, they do not seem to do anything. My mother tells me I should iron everything, including my towels, which have become hard and knobbly but, as a busy bachelor, I have neither the time nor inclination.

~

How do I fluff up towels?

To answer both of the above questions, I took expert advice from Daniel Browne, managing director of Blossom & Browne's Sycamore Laundry, specialists in antique bed linen as well as the everyday kind.

First, he says, wash your bedlinen often when it is new to get rid of the hard waxy finish put on by the makers. Regular washing will break this down and make the fabrics softer.

Next, reduce the amount of soap powder you use in the machine, especially for towels. 'Towels do not need much powder, as so much stays in them after a wash. You could wash them a second time without powder and still get a lather.' Ideally, cut the powder by half and give the towels a second, powderless wash to clear the soap.

Next, he thinks we overload our washers and tumble driers. 'Ideally, the wash should come halfway up the portal of the machine. Washing machines work by abrasion as well as soap, so tightly packed machines will not clean as well. The linen in the tumble drier should also be able to move easily.'

Finally, he does recommend fabric conditioner for a good finish. The problem is that Blossom & Browne's own conditioner, which has little scent, is not publicly available. The best solution is to shop round to find a conditioner on the market which is scented to your liking.

Or, of course, you can send the Sycamore Laundry all your washing, as they do an international postal service, especially for special old linens (020 8552 1231). Their postal service, however, may be on the expensive side if you do not live in London.

Candles and Candlesticks

I have just come back from Sweden, and I was hugely impressed at the way they used candle power. All the main hotel reception rooms were full of candles, even during the day. I would like to copy this – can you give me some ideas?

⌒

I have talked to Price's Candles (01234 264500; www.prices-candles.co.uk), which has a huge range. Perhaps the most popular candle in Sweden is the votive one, which is like an elegant night-light and burns for 11 hours. The more prosaic nightlight in the household range will last for eight hours and can be bought at Waitrose or Superdrug in bags of 25 for £4.25.

At the top of the range, you will find its beeswax versions (two dinner candles will cost £2.99 and last 10 hours) and the giant foot-high, 2¾in-wide candle (£9.99 each) will burn for no fewer than 130 hours. The long burning time means you can light them at dusk and they will keep going until well after bedtime.

Group the candles en masse, as the Swedes do, sunk into glasses, goblets or anything made of glass which will add to their glitter. Cut glass is good, for it sparkles, and putting the candles in front of mirrors doubles the strength of their light. Similarly, silver candlesticks increase the candle power – although it will not be easy to find candlesticks to fit the wide nightlights. Instead, place them on silver trays and plates, fit them into silver-based, glass hurricane lamps with larger candles grouped behind. This variation in height also seems to increase the power of the flames and adds interest to the display.

It is also great fun to collect candlesticks. We like them not to be over-ornate: Georgian silver ones, or even old Sheffield plate, are good, as are 17th-century brass prickets where the candle is impaled on a spike. Cut glass of all periods is also a winner. In each case, we also prefer our candles to be plain white and simple. Obviously, too, you must be careful not to put them near anything flammable and to check they cannot be knocked over easily.

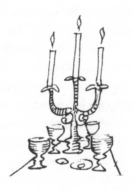

Washing Cashmere

Although I have read on the internet that one can hand-wash cashmere items and the label of my cashmere jacket indicates machine washing, all of my cashmere sweaters recommend dry cleaning. Which is correct?

～

We rather agree with you about this cashmere confusion. Sometimes cashmere says 'wash' and sometimes 'dry clean' and we are suspicious that those manufacturers which suggest dry cleaning are doing it to avoid being sued if things go wrong in the wash. It is, is it not, easier always to suggest the less risky but more expensive option?

Here, we take a pragmatic view on whether to wash or dry clean. First, we would never wash any cashmere but knitted garments so, if your jacket is, say, a tweed or worsted made of cashmere, then take it to the dry cleaner, whatever it says on the label. If, however, it is a jersey jacket, then perhaps you should do what it tells you.

On sweaters, we take the risk on most and wash them in a special cashmere-and-wool washing liquid which is extra gentle and on the wool cycle in the machine. We have had no trouble – we dry them flat on one of those pulleys you find in country houses, and then give them a very light ironing if they are at all creased.

That having been said, all our cashmeres are plain knits and of a single colour. I would be less happy to machine wash any multi-coloured knits or those involving frou-frou lace, fancy patterns or extremely fragile threads. Really, it is for you to make your own decision on the quality and toughness of each individual piece and, if it is something hugely valuable or a great favourite, err on the cautious side.

Re-Surfacing a Bath

I would be very grateful if you could tell me where we could get a bath re-surfaced.

The firm you should contact is Renubath (0800 138 2202), which offers three different grades of re-surfacing – in situ, of course. The three-star service will take five days to cure; the four-star has the surface artificially dried for you in two hours; the five-star deluxe service gives the bath a double coating, which is then dried and polished. It has a two-year guarantee.

Renubath has given me prices, which include travel to your home in Staffordshire: three-star will be £185 plus VAT; four-star is an extra £40 plus VAT; and the full five-star service is a total of £320 plus VAT. I hope your bath has a long and happy second life.

Cleaning Wool Mattresses and Pillows

I am married to an Italian and we lived in Italy for some time where we used both wool mattresses and pillows. They have craftsmen there who will undo them, clean the wool, tease it and put it all back together again. There is such place just off the Boulevard St Germain in Paris. Have you heard of a place in Great Britain?

⤳

Yes, I think you are in luck. Nu-Life Upholstery Repairs, 17, Chepstow Corner, 1 Pembridge Villas, London w2 (020 7221 1515) will remake and recover your old wool mattress – and many other things besides. Mr Marlow recommends that you telephone and talk it over with him so he can give you a price.

Maintaining Household Supplies

My daughter has started to share a flat in London with three other people. She is constantly complaining that they run out of essential supplies – salt, kitchen paper, washing-up liquid – because none of the four of them will take responsibility (or, if they do, no one tells them when supplies are exhausted). Do you have a simple solution?

～

Yes, I do, although it does need an element of responsibility to work. It is an updated version of a rather nifty Victorian gadget called the Household Wants Indicator. This consisted of a plain board that lists all likely supplies a household may need. In Victorian times, necessary items included burning oil, hearthstone and turpentine. The board also has a series of small metal buttons, one beside each product, which can be flipped to show which products are running low. Your daughter's flatmates need to get together and list all of their wants. These are not, of course, the special items such as lemongrass and couscous which can be bought as needed. Rather, these are long-term supplies that make daily life possible, such as soap, ground coffee, bread, eggs and lightbulbs.

Assuming that one or all of the flatmates have access to a computer (and who does not nowadays?), the finished list should be typed and printed out in a large typeface. Next, get this sheet laminated for long-term wear, and hang it up by the front door. When supplies are getting low or they have been completely exhausted, one flatmate should put a small red sticker or Post-it note beside the products needed. This is where responsibility comes in: the four must make an agreement about how the shopping is to be done and how it is paid for. Depending on the agreement reached, whoever is in charge of the next shopping trip should add the red-sticker products to their list. When the items have been bought, then the stickers should be removed. It is important that the four flatmates work out a system between themselves and, if one flatmate is notoriously scatty, it is best to leave him or her out of the system altogether.

Cleaning Chemists' Jars

We have tried using double-strength Steradent and leaving full-strength bleach in our Victorian glass pharmacy jars for several days, but still the cloudy stains inside remain. In one case, the glass stopper cannot be removed. We have left it in very hot water for a time and we have buried it in ice cubes. We have also tried to get olive oil to seep in, but to no avail. Have you any other suggestions?

⌒

This is the edited reply that I gave to someone with the same problems – although their problem was with a decanter: I have talked to the British Antique Dealers' Association (BADA) and they say that if the decanter is stained darkly, then a good bottle brush and hot water with a dash of Cif or Astonish might do the trick. But it sounds as if your piece has gone milky, which may be caused by not drying it fully after washing up. If this is the case, BADA says that it may be possible for a professional to buff it up inside.

If you would like to do the work yourself (and be warned this may damage your piece beyond help), you will find details of the considerable amount of equipment you need for the job at www.great-glass.co.uk.

It sounds as if the stuck stopper is also a professional's job. BADA recommends one of its members, the antique glass specialist W. G. T. Burne (020 8543 6319).

If using its services is difficult for you – the company is based in London – you might try asking your local museum if they have a repairer on their books. Sorry not to have an easy DIY remedy, but it seems you have tried the most obvious ones.

A Gift for a Researcher

I have arranged to go and visit a complete stranger who has some archives relevant to my own family. He has been very kind and offered me a day's search of them, plus lunch. Should I bring him a gift to show my appreciation?

No, I don't think you need to, if your helper is also interested in research. We find that there is a camaraderie among researchers, who will happily help out as long as it doesn't conflict with their own work – that's when they become dragons protecting their treasure. Variously, we have had an architectural historian who called to say he had found a plan of a house drawn by a 19th-century family member, which 'could be winkled out from' the offices that retained it; another tracked down and arranged photographs of buildings by the same architect in her city; and a third took photographs of a family monument in Zomba, in Malawi, when he happened, quite by accident, to be passing. All these were worth far more than a bottle of wine or bunch of flowers. However, if you have no treasure to give your researcher, then a bottle of wine or something a bit more imaginative would be in order.

Choosing the Perfect Nanny

I need to employ a nanny. Can you give me any help on how go about choosing one?

❧

This is an extremely important decision: whether to have a nanny and how to find someone just right for you. I therefore spoke to Clare Dent, the agency manager of the Norland Nursery Training College in Bath – the *ne plus ultra* of nanny colleges. Obviously, she believes that a Norlander is the best you can get, because the agency, which supplies permanent, temporary and overseas nannies, only has nannies on its books who have trained there and have passed the college's scheme. 'We can vouch for all our nannies because we know them. No one who has not completed a course will be on our agency's books.'

Their nannies cost from £13,000 a year for a probationer (one who has completed the formal training, but needs to spend a year learning the practicalities with a real family) and a day nanny will be about £80 to £100 per day.

In general, however, she advises that you should decide if and what kind of cover you want first. You may find you don't need a full-time nanny, but something less permanent. To begin your search, you should go to a reputable agency: nannies from the REC (Recreation and Employment Confederation, www.rec.co.uk) must abide by its codes of conduct and should, therefore, be safe.

Next, you should check their qualifications and references, both of which are very important, and that each nanny is who she says she is. When this is done, call your choices in for a short interview. It is most important here to make sure you actually like the prospective nanny – no matter what her qualifications are: if you don't get on, then don't consider her. 'You will never be able to discuss things properly with someone you don't like.'

After this interview, make a shortlist and ask those on it back for a further interview, which should take about half a day. During this time, let each candidate and the children spend time together to see whether they all get on and you like her style.

'Look for someone calm, friendly and with a sense of fun,' says Clare Dent. 'It doesn't matter whether she is 18 or 60, as long as she is fit and healthy.'

Bathroom Soaps

My wife is constantly looking for a soap, for use in the bath-room, that will leave a nice scent when it is used. The perfumes from all of the soaps she has tried leave a barely detectable smell, including a quite expensive one which was recommended.

～

On the whole, you will need to buy a more expensive soap because the makers care about the scent lasting all the way through. Soaps are very personal, and we tend to like natural, herby scents. So, we use the following: Trevarno's natural lavender or cedar and citrus hand-made soap (www. trevarno.co.uk for mail order); geranium or lavender bath bricks from Arran Aromatics (www.arran-aromatics.co.uk, also mail order); Roger et Gallet's sandalwood or fern, from most good chemists; and glycerine soap from Waitrose, in unusual flavours such as mango juice; cucumber and wild mint; and redcurrant and cassis. Pears soap should never be ignored, either.

Removing Water Marks from Furniture

I have discovered two water marks on a mahogany table, possibly drips from flowers on a plant. Is there any way I can remove them?

～

Assuming that your table has not been French polished (in which case there is no remedy other than French polishing it again), your best bet is to spread a small amount of raw linseed oil on the spots, rub well in, and give it about a week to sink in. This should darken the spotted area to match the original.

If this does not work, reapply and leave for another few days. When you are satisfied that the spots are as removed as possible, polish the whole with a beeswax furniture polish.

The combination of linseed oil and beeswax polish will remove the spots, and should then bring the wood back to its original shine.

New Use for a Cake Stand

I own a lovely glass cake stand. It is finely cut, has three tiers and stands about 18in high. It is also now unfashionable. Can you suggest a new way to use it?

∾

Just think of it as a display stand instead. You can employ it on a table to serve various nibbles at the start of a meal: skewered shrimps, sushi, shot glasses full of cold soup and tiny rolls of smoked salmon, for instance. Or, at the end of a meal, cheese, grapes, butter and biscuits. If it is as lovely as you say, it will make the table look special.

Elsewhere, you could use it in the bathroom for soaps, Q-tips and cotton wool or on the hall table for notes, letters, cards and memos.

Removing Lily Pollen Stains

I have just been to a wedding, where the massed ranks of lilies shed quantities of red pollen all over my lovely black coat. Can you suggest ways to get rid of it?

I do wish people would not use these lilies without cutting off the stamens with their disfiguring pollen: so many clothes have been damaged by them. From trial and error, I suggest that you should try putting Sellotape over the powder stains, which will, with luck, pick off the loose pollen. Keep dabbing the tape over the marks until they have gone.

Incidentally, Sellotape can also be used to remove other kinds of dust – but never, ever, stick together old and valuable documents with it. Over the years, it will stain the paper a nasty yellow, which can never be removed.

Dealing with Damaged Carpets

My study is covered with an old oriental carpet. It has now developed so many holes that people keep tripping over them and falling onto my piles of books, bruising themselves and disarranging my volumes, which is most annoying. Can I get the carpet repaired?

∽

P robably not, because the carpet will be weak even where there are no holes, so the repairs will simply break up the rest of the weave.

You could, of course, try the solution of one distinguished academic, who put a copy of *Country Life* over each hole, thus alerting visitors and yourself to the dangers.

Otherwise, perhaps a new old oriental carpet is the answer. Watch out for them at country-house car-boot sales, country-house auctions and lesser antique shops.

Red Wine on a Dress

What do I do about spilt red wine on my silk evening dress?

⤳

We have asked the expert cleaners at Peters & Falla, on London's New Kings Road (020 7731 3255) what should be done. They are absolutely adamant that you must not put anything on the stain. Because dry-cleaners use chemicals, they need to know what they are working on. If it is just red wine, they can use the appropriate chemical, but if you have poured white wine, or even fizzy water, over the top, then they have to fight to get that out as well. This applies to any horrible stain, on any material.

Peters & Falla say, difficult as it is to leave well alone, you must. Don't mess with the marks, and get it to a dry-cleaner as soon as you can.

We have experience: someone had their wedding dress covered with chocolate cake. They carefully left the stain, and took it to the dry-cleaners on the Monday morning. There is absolutely no evidence of it now.

Care of Unvarnished Pine

I have a large farmhouse table with a top of unvarnished pine. I would really love it to look pale and interesting, as if I scrubbed it daily (which, of course, I don't). Any suggestions?

⌇

You should try Scandinavian Woodcare products, made in a country where they know all about pale furniture. The products are actually intended for floors (which also look splendid when soft white). You will need, initially, a bottle of its lye, which will bleach the table top to the characteristic yellow colour of pine, and a bottle of its white soap, which should be applied to the bleached and scoured surface. It will soften, whiten and add a slight shine to the already bleached planks. This soap should be used whenever the table needs it. Eva Johnson (01638 797773) imports Scandinavian Woodcare products to Britain and, when you order from her, she will send a very helpful instruction leaflet. She also suggests using a sealing oil for your table top.

The soap is £9.50 a litre (or £35 for five litres), and the lye is £11.50 a litre.

What to Do About Upside-Down Wallpaper

I stupidly went on holiday leaving my decorator to rewall-paper the living room. When I got back, he had put the paper – with a design of red cherries hanging from twigs and green leaves – on upside down. Can I sue him? What do you suggest?

∾

I would not sue him, as it will almost certainly cost you more than repapering the room – not to mention the stress involved. I also disapprove of this constant suing when things go wrong.

My suggestion is that you should strike a blow for eccentricity. Tell anyone who visits that you prefer the design to be upside down, and that you asked your decorator (despite his protests) to hang it that way. Mention that you have taken a leaf from the German artist Baselitz (born 1938), who deliberately painted most of his figures and images upside down. In this way, you will appear to be unconventional, interested in design and knowledgeable about modern art.

Roller Towels

I cannot think I am the only Country Life *reader with a roller towel in my utility room. I badly need new ones, but, ask as I have, I am unable to find a supplier. Can you help?*

❧

Yes, Pedlars (01330 850400; www.pedlars.co.uk) sells roller towels. They cost £11.50 and are either natural or striped with blue, red or green. They are 85% cotton.

Alternatively, Lakeland (01539 488100) sells them. In a blue-checked towelling, 100% cotton, they cost £8.99.

Care of a Stuffed Otter

I have a stuffed otter in my living room, which is not in a glass case, and I am afraid that, in time, the fur might dry out or crack. Should I be treating it to keep it supple? I love the advice you give in Country Life, *and look forward to your reply.*

∽

I asked a top taxidermist, and he says that, if the otter has been properly stuffed, you should have no problems. It should last at least a century, if not longer. To maintain your otter, keep it dust free by using a hairdryer blowing cold (this is also a good idea for any fragile dusting). Also, keep it out of sunlight.

There is no need to keep it in a glass case unless the animal was stuffed in the 19th century, in which case, arsenic may have been used, which can still be dangerous. It's also a question of taste: the glass case may look better in your view or not so good and will still have to be dusted. Of course, if it hasn't been stuffed properly, you will be in trouble.

Fabric Box Files

I have just redesigned my home office in shades of black and beige with steel handles and fittings. What I now need is a series of box files that will match. Those available at most office shops are quite awful – primary colours, shiny plastic, cheap styles. Can you suggest somewhere I can get fabric filing boxes in suitable colours?

～

You can start with the Conran shop, which usually has a few filing boxes and stationery in plain black fabric (check they are in stock first). Failing that, Kate Forman (01962 732244; www.kateforman.co.uk) makes up box files, wastepaper baskets and address books in various fabrics. I like striped cotton in beige and black: very efficient and chic.

Organising Your Office

I have recently retired as the chairman of a large company and, without my personal assistants and various minions, I find it terribly difficult to keep control of my appointments and phone messages. Have you any suggestions?

～

Yes, what you need is extremely simple and very effective. Buy a book-sized bound notebook, making sure that it will open flat and not close if you take your hand off it. Use this to record all – and I do mean all – your telephone conversations with the date at the top of each. Make notes as you talk of any decision, any appointment, any address, email or phone numbers. This will not only remind you of what the call was about and when you made it, it will also act as a record.

Thus, if you ring your local council and ask for a second dustbin, when nothing happens (as will probably be the case), you can ring again and tell them to speed up, quoting your previous telephone call.

In another example, I know a man who rang to say his house had been missed off the rating list (very honest). Amazingly, nothing happened in this case either. So, when he telephoned a second and third time, and finally they came back with a bill for £9,000 in total, he was able to point out their inefficiency with exact dates of his calls and so be allowed to pay in instalments.

A Parking Problem

I live in a London square where parking is severely restricted. My next-door neighbour, who has a large and ugly 4x4 with a disabled sticker, parks it in front of my windows every day, leaving her own clear. I know of no one in the house who is disabled and am getting increasingly annoyed by her thoughtlessness. Should I inform the parking authorities or ask her to leave my own views clear?

⌒

I am sorry to say this, but you should do neither – you must suffer in silence. I know, I know, it is infuriating, and it is extremely rude of your neighbour to park in front of your house rather than her own. But imagine the scenario if you take offensive action: you will have a neighbour with an enduring grudge, even if you just ask her to shift the wretched hulk and park it elsewhere. If you read the papers carefully, you will see that there is no one more likely to go to law or become violent than a neighbour who resents you. They slit your tyres, tell the council when you water your garden and, I am not joking, resort to murder.

Try to minimise the grudge you bear, hope they will move soon and consider how you may be annoying them. This is one time where turning the other cheek is the smart option.

Buying Traditional White Shirts

I always wear plain, white, cotton shirts, long sleeved, no
nonsense, without button-down collars and a quite sporty
cut. As I don't have to go into an office, I don't need to
wear suits or ties. All my shirts are beginning to collapse
and I cannot find new ones to this – I would have thought
– simple specification. Do you know a source?

W hy do so many nice plain shirts have short sleeves?
Or button-down collars? What are they buttoning
down? Surely they are an unfortunate American import, created in the land of tornadoes, where collars might need extra
support. Boden could help: its catalogue has an Architect
Shirt. It is 100% cotton, semi-fitted, with a nice, plain collar.
There are six versions, including pure white. Sizes from small
to XXL, price £45. Order online at www.boden.co.uk or telephone 0845 677 5000.

How to Decorate Inexpensively

I have just bought my first flat and am now penniless. Do you have good ideas for decorating on a pittance?

⌇

The places to start are car-boot sales, flea markets and antique markets. For furniture, look out for sturdy pieces with good lines. If their condition is dicey, paint them – a greyish white is good, and better still if given a coating of beeswax. On the walls, you can put large pieces of fabric instead of pictures – distressed *toile de Jouy*, moth-eaten Paisley shawls and so on, which can also be used as throws or, if grotty, cut up into cushion covers.

Paint your floors a slightly darker off-white than the furniture so rugs and carpets are hardly needed. Skips can be an amazing source – especially in fancy areas such as Chelsea, Edinburgh New Town or Bath. Keep rummaging.

Watch out for black-and-white prints of good quality. You can get whole sets at £1 each, which can be nailed up in groups rather than framed.

It's a good idea to have a monochrome scheme so everything matches, then add colour for emphasis. Multiples always work: watch out for good labels, such as Worcestershire sauce, Marmite or old-fashioned chemists' bottles, and array them in rows. Pebbles and shells are free and, if well chosen to be similar in size and marking, are wonderful in bowls or shelves.

Start a collection of objects no one wants: sailing ships on fire screens embroidered by great aunts, pictures by amateurs who can't paint, wonky ceramics: en masse, they become eccentrically pleasing. Decorate with food, such as oranges and lemons, which you can then eat. Carrot leaves look good in glass jars. I hope you've got the message: dare to be different, invent your own style, which, if it works, no one will realise is driven by desperation.

Guests Who Break Glasses

I have a holiday cottage, and I am in despair at the number of wine glasses that get broken. Not even only in orgies, but every day. What's wrong with these people – is it simply that they can't live without a dishwasher?

~

I feel sure that people are a lot less clumsy with their own objects than they are with other people's – especially as many will vanish into the night without confessing the damage they have done. We have found, in our holiday lets, smashed casserole dishes pieced together and hidden under others, not to mention chips with everything.

With wine glasses, you cannot go wrong with the petit ballon which was used for wine in the Paris bistros of the 1920s. It is heavyweight, machine-made and ordinary-wine-glass shaped. We have tried it out and, so far, have had no chips or breakages. You can buy sets of six (€10.50) from www.manufactum.co.uk, an excellent German firm selling practical and unusual household and other goods.

Selling Linen

I would like to know if there is any market for absolutely top-quality table linen (around 1950), lace tablecloths and so on.

～

I am not clear whether you want to buy or sell table linen, but I have to say that there is a buyer's market because the best table linen, second-hand, is not much sought after. I think it should be, because not only is it far better than most of today's linen, it is also a great deal cheaper. The trouble is that many people do not use tablecloths, especially lace, which is not fashionable. If you must sell it, try a local antiques market where there may be a specialist fabric stall. But it would be better to keep it in a drawer until prices improve.

Electric Fans

*Being well-organised and practical, I am already plan-
ning for the baking weather prophesied for the summer.
I intend to buy some electric fans while there is still a
chance of snow so, surely, they will not have sold out. Any
suggestions?*

༄

Office suppliers Viking Direct (www.viking-direct.co.
uk; 0844 412 0000) have a fair selection, priced from
£9.39 for a clip-on desk fan in plastic to chrome pedestal fans
in two heights. One, the smaller, is £23.49 and the taller is
£46.99. Both will oscillate and have three speeds. Lakeland
(www.lakeland.co.uk; 01539 488100) have a high-velocity
air circulator with three speeds (£39.99) and one with beech-
wood effect blades. The company stocks a remote control
tower fan, £59.99, which is, it says, extremely quiet and good
in bedrooms. It also has a remote control, eight-hour timer
and 'natural breeze' mode, whatever that is.

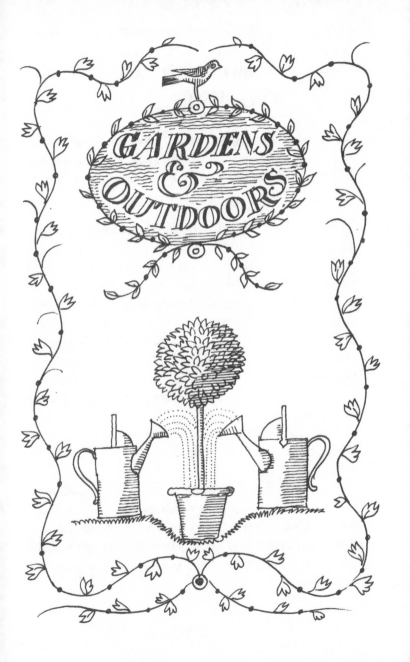

GARDENS & OUTDOORS

Lawnmowers and
Their Different Uses

My husband already has four different machines for cutting the grass in our – admittedly large – garden. He now tells me that he needs a fifth. Is he right or is it toys for boys?

〜

I am afraid that he may well be right, depending on the type of garden and the type of grass that you have. Our head gardener has at least that many machines: he swears he needs different machines for different parts of the garden.

First, there is a motorised cylinder mower that is essential for a good lawn. One with a 24in set of blades is probably needed for a big lawn, and it will pick up the cuttings and make a good stripe (Robert Tomlinson, of Tomlinson Groundcare in Suffolk, tells me that a roller rotary mower is even better for stripes). The cylinder mower will cost about £2,300 new.

Next, the gardeners need a Flymo because it is ideal for sloping banks – nothing else other than a scythe will do. This will cost about £400.

A lawn tractor with cutting equipment is important if you have large areas of grass which are to be cut, although not to such a high standard as the lawn. This can cost anything from £1,750 to £10,000. Mr Tomlinson says that the trend is to get bigger machines and the £10,000 tractor is a best seller.

Then, of course, a garden that allows the long grass to grow in spring for the pleasure of blossoming cow parsley will need a heavy-duty long-grass cutter when the display is over. This will cost about £3,000. And finally, a strimmer will trim the nooks and crannies. Its price is a mere £200 to £400. This means, if your husband goes for the big lawn tractor, his machines will cost a total of £16,000. Or you could move to Germany, where, Mr Tomlinson says, they don't do borders and they don't care for fancy lawns.

Black Metal Fencing

We have just let our large field to a local farmer for his cattle. I am keen to fence off a portion so we can walk round to parts of our garden, and we want to use un-obtrusive black metal fencing – the sort you see in parks and large estates – rather than the traditional post-and-rail. Short of approaching the Duchess of Devonshire to find out her supplier, so far I have had no luck. Any suggestions?

～

We were keen here to do exactly as you want to, and, although we did not approach the Duchess, further enquiries turned up the firm Paddock Fencing of Peterborough (01733 270580).

It makes two different types of estate fencing: the first is pre-made in 2m lengths with a round rail top and flat bars of steel below. At one end there's a prong to knock into the ground; the other prongless end connects with the next length with its own prong – and you can bolt them together. It is supplied and painted, but you have to install it yourself.

The snag with this system is that it will not cope with sloping ground, because the panels are rigid (slight undulations are all right). For less level ground, you must have the continuous fencing which comes in 5m lengths. It consists of poles to knock into the ground and bars of steel to slot through horizontally. It comes undercoated but without a top coat, because paint would be damaged during installation. The price is £35 + VAT a metre.

Toni Butcher, a partner of Paddock Fencing, says 'The premade sections are more popular because they are easy to install.' The firm also makes bespoke fencing to suit any situation, and a series of metal gates to match. These cost from £178 for a 1m gate or £340 for one of 3.5m, both plus VAT. As you will see, this is not a cheap option compared to post-and-rail, but much more elegant and extremely long-lasting.

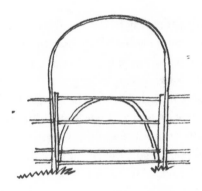

Water Features

The past few hot weeks of August have convinced me that I should have the sound of splashing water in my garden, just to make me feel cooler. The garden is small and has high walls down each side. Ideally, I would like a trough fed by a wall-mounted spout. How can I do this?

⌣

It is actually quite easy to create a water feature on a wall, as long as you have electricity near by (you don't need a source of water funnily enough). First, you should buy a black plastic trough about four feet by two, and three feet deep. Position it against your chosen garden wall, which needs to be five or six feet high. Now hide the whole tank with decorative outer brick, flint or painted concrete wall, which should be elegant but not too fancy.

You will then need to buy a submersible pump (between £25 and £55 and the size of a box of chocolates) which should be connected to a hidden electric power source (near the bottom of the wall, behind an evergreen plant?) via a waterproof electric wire. This will lie on the trough's bottom sucking in water and pumping it to the ornamental spout attached to the wall. This is done via a length of thin black plastic pipe attached at one end to the pump and threaded through the backing wall below the water level. The other end of the pipe, concealed in or behind the wall, should be attached to the back of the ornamental spout. I recommend a plain lead star or Adam style lead sheep's mask from a specialist supplier.

Fill the black tank almost to the top with your garden hose, making sure that the water covers all the works. This whole idea is to make your spout look as though the stream of cool fresh water splashing into the trough comes from mountain spring water, rather than being shoved round endlessly by an electric pump. This is why it is essential to have everything in black plastic and don't even think about turquoise blue.

Clock Towers

I have a rather undistinguished outbuilding – it was some kind of shed – but it is in a crucial position in the garden. I want to use it as an eye-catcher and think it would be a good idea to make it into a clock tower. Obviously, any clock would have to tell the time and, as the tower would be on the roof, I wonder if it's possible to buy a good-looking electric clock instead of having to wind the mechanism every few days. Please advise.

～

Curiously, we have gone through exactly this experience, turning an old farm office into an ornamental lodge with a clock tower that gives those working in the garden the exact time to knock off for lunch. Our tower is four-sided but, to reduce expense, we decided to put the clocks on only two sides of the edifice and leave the other two blank.

Good Directions (01489 797773), the company we used, will sell cupolas in all sorts of designs and sizes, but we preferred to build our own in order to get the proportions right (at height, the right size – usually bigger than you imagine is crucial.)

The company sells clock faces with Arabic and Roman numerals, with skeleton faces and in medieval and Art Deco styles. We preferred numerals in gold leaf on an azure blue background; our clock faces and their electric motors were 790mm across and each cost £650 plus VAT. Motorless dummy faces are available for £280 plus VAT. You can also buy a contraption which will automatically adjust to summertime and Greenwich meantime changes (called a resychroniser) and costing £380 plus VAT or a battery version (£490 plus VAT) which will keep the clock going during power failures. Even without these, because the works are electric, you do not need to climb up ladders but simply stop or start the switch.

When the clock is ready to go, it is crucial that each face is exactly synchronised. I suggest you organise this at midday and make sure both hour and minute hand are placed identically – otherwise, of course, your workers will knock off for lunch at different times. We found the clocks expensive, but they have worked without any problem for seven years.

Two Ways to Deal with Fallen Leaves

I am desperate to know how to deal with fallen leaves. Last year, our garden turned into a slippery wet mush when autumn came, and the lawn took ages to recover from the rotting leaves. I have to admit we were lazy but we have learnt our lesson this year.

∽

The first question about fallen leaves is whether you need to pick them up at all. If the autumn is fine and dry with a breeze then you can leave the leaves (so to speak) to blow themselves into a handy corner ready for collecting. They will not go mushy or slippery. Once they are cornered, then two pieces of plywood or hardboard, roughly 12in by 9in, make handy pincers for picking them up in quantity.

If on the other hand, the weather is wet or you cannot bear the temporary untidiness, then the best implement for a large garden is an electric blower-cum-vacuum – the sort you will often see workers using in municipal parks. Blow the leaves into a pile then pick up all the bits with the pincers (the vacuum will probably take longer but, crucially it rarely sucks up gravel). As a vacuum, this machine is also useful at other times for tidying hedge and grass trimmings or neatening formal areas, for example. Stihl's BG55 (£210 from Charterhouse Richmond, 0845 458 2599) will do the job well if you have the vacuum attachment. The leaves are shredded to make useful mulch.

If your garden is smaller, then a purpose-designed rake is the answer. Chelwood rakes (from LBS 0870 727 3616) have three good ones. The Landscraper is 28in wide with strong steel teeth and a back edge for grading and levelling ground. Chelwood also makes two 25in-wide polyproplene rakes. Model 32P has a shark-like number of teeth, which pick up leaves. A special device allows the rake to be turned and the leaves dropped into a sack or barrow. There is also Model 16P, which is a modern version of the old hay rake, with wide spaced teeth.

When the leaves are all collected, put them into a special composter. Rotted leaf makes excellent mulch, keeping weeds down as it fertilises.

I dread the arrival of autumn because, even though our garden is not big, we are surrounded by deciduous trees. As the leaves drop, paths get slippery and the flowerbeds look like compost heaps. Raking the leaves is boring and arduous and destroys many of the plants in the beds. Have you a solution?

Yes, of course. You must buy yourself a garden vacuum cleaner, the kind you may have noticed the parks departments in towns employ. This will probably cost between £50 and £80, so the expense is not outrageous and I can assure you that you will never regret the outlay.

The garden vacuum is exactly what you would expect in that it has a large nozzle for sucking up the leaves and a huge bag for collecting them as you work. The strength of the sucking mechanism is finely balanced so that the machine will pick up dead leaves and small twigs without disturbing the gravel or, indeed, the plants in your beds.

The machine can also be switched to blow instead of suck and this allows you to marshal all the debris you want to collect into a tight, easy corner rather than vacuuming the entire garden.

With some of the pricier versions (such as the Ryobi), the machine will also mulch the leaves and twigs so that they can be spread round the plants or left to turn into leaf-mould. Nor does the vacuum sit uselessly in the potting shed all summer: it is excellent for doing a quick tidy if you have an open garden day or an alfresco party.

The only drawback to these devices is that they work with electricity and therefore must be plugged in some-where – but the purchase of a good extension lead should sort that out.

Bonfires

I know it sounds hopeless but I cannot light a good bonfire. It spurts up all right but, as soon as I turn my back, it just goes out, leaving a huge pile of debris around a central burnt area. What am I doing wrong?

⌇

I have consulted the head gardener and he tells me that it is essential to build up a good core and, also, not to turn your back on the fire for at least 30 minutes. When you start a bonfire, the first thing is to clear an area about a yard across down to the ground where you will light the fire. It is no good just putting a match to any old heap and hoping for the best. When the ground is cleared, make the beginnings of a fire by crumpling newspaper sheets (oh, the uses of newspapers), topping them with flattened cardboard cartons – just jump heavily on them. On top of the old cartons add some old pieces of dry wood.

Then light the newspaper and wait until the whole edifice is burning nicely – the paper goes up first and lasts long enough to light the cartons which in turn set the wood aflame. When you have a good, vigorous blaze, start putting bonfire material on in amounts small enough to catch fire rather than put it out. As each pitchforkful catches fire, add more small amounts, beating them down, so no gap appears between the fire and waiting burnables.

As well as a pitchfork, you should have a stout, straight branch for poking into the fire to avoid that gap. It may take half an hour to get to this point but, by now, the bonfire should have its good core and you can load on rather more and leave it for some time.

A bonfire with a good burning core can stay alight all night, or for several days and can even cope with a downpour. Just keep feeding it until everything is burnt and the resultant ash can be used to fertilise your raspberry canes.

Custom-Made Baskets

I have just bought a charming old cottage and am plan-
ning to design a charming old kitchen. My idea — not
particularly original, I agree — is to use baskets instead of
drawers to hold cutlery, vegetables, wooden spoons etc.
Because the room is far from regular in shape, I will have
to get these made specially to fit. Can you advise?

∽

O f course – advice is my middle name. Basketmaking is
one of the few crafts that has not just succumbed to
machinery – they continue to be as handmade as they were
in the 13th century and, as a result, it is no more expensive
to have one custom-made than to buy off the shelf.

England still has its own basketmaking area: the Somerset
Levels wetland is the perfect site for growing withy, the
special willow cultivated for baskets. The Coate family have
been growing these willows and weaving them into baskets
since 1819, and at Coates Willows and Wetlands Centre,
based at Stoke St Gregory in the heart of the Levels, you can
see how the growing branches are harvested, dried and
woven. More to the point, you can order a basket of your
choice, made to fit your new kitchen.

The most useful, I think, would be rectangular baskets of
between 5in and 9in high (depending on their intended use),
somewhat like a large in-tray which is woven with a neat
gap at the top so you can easily pull them out. They can be
bought in dark brown, bleached beige and tan. A 5in-high

version will cost you about £25 – no more than off-the-peg baskets displayed in the Coates shop. The firm will also make basket for mail order.

www.coates-willowbaskets.co.uk

Decorating a House by the Water

Our new house abuts directly onto a waterway. How does one redecorate all the outside? (The previous owners do not know as they never decorated – hence we now need to.) Have you any suggestions?

This is a tricky one. I have asked round, however, and think I can help. The obvious solution is scaffolding. But if your water is deep and the bottom too soft, scaffolders will not be happy to oblige. They could cantilever the scaffold poles through the windows but this might put too much pressure on the house's walls.

Where the water is not that wide – a stream or narrow river or canal – then some decorators can work from the basket of a cherry picker. If the water is wide, then the reach will defeat all but the most enormous cranes and you may find it hard to get one of these locally. To bring one from elsewhere is hugely expensive.

A window cleaner, working on buildings by the Thames, has provided the solution. He uses a pontoon or raft. This works best when the water is still and, obviously, not too tidal, but he says if he watches out for motorboats and barges, he can avoid the rocking their wash causes. Equally, he works only on calm days.

Another acquaintance has experimented with rafts: his is made in three parts so it can be lifted and stored. Each part has wooden boards screwed onto a frame holding four large empty oil drums (for buoyancy). When the three are put together, the total size is 6ft x 8ft. My adviser says that the house should have metal eyes screwed into its walls 6ft apart at the level of the raft. These can be left permanently in place. The raft also has four eyes. The idea is to secure the raft firmly by tying a rope round these links to four in the house walls. Two would probably do, but, if one failed, there could be a nasty accident if you are up a ladder. The foot of the ladder, by the way, is held against a baton nailed to the raft floor to stop it slipping. When all the parts are put together and operational, the raft can be punted into place or, if the pond bottom is too deep, paddled like an Indian canoe. Alternatively, a small outboard motor would work.

Building a Drystone Wall

I would like to try to build a drystone wall. How should I go about it?

❧

I t may sound obvious, but first you should make sure your property is in an area with plenty of stones, such as the Pennines or Lake District. Drystone walling was invented to use up all those random pieces of rock scattered round unfertile fields while also giving them boundaries. Such work in unstony areas, such as Suffolk, or in ones where the only available rocks are rounded cobbles would be unnecessarily expensive and out of keeping. The best way to learn the technique is to watch an expert, as we did with Clifford Horsefield up in the Pennines. Failing that, here are some pointers.

The wall should consist of two separate walls, set on a batter (the base wider than the top) with a gap of a few inches between them. This is to be filled with small stones, rubble and compacted clay (you can use cement, but this does not qualify as a drystone wall).

The foundations should be started about six inches below the soil level. Large stones, like quoins, should be arranged at each end, to hold up the whole. Select each stone in the wall to fit like a jigsaw and ensure, if necessary by packing small stones beneath, that it does not rock. It is essential that each stone is properly bedded. Do not be tempted to think the stone above will do the job. It will not. Generally, the base should be of larger stones than the top but, as the wall rises by a foot, you should place large, flat stones bridging each of the two walls every three or four feet. This gives stability and joins the two elements.

As the wall rises, add the central filling. When you have reached about five feet – drystone walls are unlikely to work much higher – top the whole edifice with selected stones set upright and crosswise to the main wall as neatly as you can. Drystone walling is highly physical (better exercise than the gym) and extremely satisfying, so good luck.

When Bamboo Takes Over

About five years ago, I planted a dwarf bamboo for ground cover in a stream-side bed. Since then, it has entirely taken over the bed – well, I suppose that's what I thought I wanted – and it is threatening to take over the stream, the garden, the universe. I have attacked it with a fork and spade but it is almost impossible to divide. Help, please, before we, too, vanish in its clutches.

୰

Many bamboos are known thugs – and that is not just the tall, imposing ones. The plant's root system is similar to couch grass, which means that it will run underground, through hedges, under paths and, as you say, across water. You have obviously planted your dwarf version in a prime site – most bamboos love damp, fertile ground. Because the root system is so tough, an ordinary, large garden fork or spade will make little impression on bamboo and exhaust you in the process.

Many desperate gardeners will take an axe to bamboo and this works fine. However, you might like to invest in Sneeboer's Narrow Spade (£68) which is specially designed to chop through the tough roots of shrubs. It has a long, wooden handle and the stainless-steel blade is narrow, in the style of a peat cutter. The extremely sharp base has a tri-angle cut from it at the bottom to gather the roots together and, where it meets the ash shaft, the shoulders are widened so you can jump on them, adding extra pressure to the blade, which is double-riveted to the shaft on both sides.

Because it is both narrow and sharp, this tool is just the job for slicing through bamboo roots.

You will, however, need both a large fork and spade too – the spade if you want to dig out and preserve the chunks of bamboo and the fork if you want to get out the unwanted roots completely. Bamboo roots left in the soil will probably grow again. Finally, if you love bamboo despite its bullying habits, plant it in a large, hidden container so as to control the root runs.

Specialist gardening tools can be bought in most top garden shops but, for mail order, try Manufactum (0800 096 0937; www.manufactum.co.uk). They charge £4.95 delivery on each order.

Alternatives to Grass

We have a very small town garden with walls on all sides. It currently has a central lawn but this is clearly impractical. In winter, even if we walk over it rarely, it becomes muddy and ugly. In summer, the grass goes brown and the soil cracks. What should we do?

～

I have long believed that small gardens are better off without lawns, especially in inner cities, where they rarely thrive. There are plenty of other options for you. I assume that you have perennials and shrubs at the edges of the plot and the lawn is in the centre. If this is the case, you can remove the lawn entirely and create, effectively, a single large bed. The cheapest way to do this is to cover the entire garden area, including the beds, with a mulch of loose bark. Let the plants in the beds spread out – and many will readily seed in the bark – until the whole plot is one large planted area.

You will probably want paths among the plants, either informally meandering or squared off and formal. If you need to sit out in the garden, create a central, unplanted area with plants surrounding it.

Exactly the same can be done with gravel, a rather more expensive and elegant option. Make sure that you choose a small pea gravel in as light a shade as you can find, for this will feel lighter and more sunny. Again, you can create formal or informal paths among the beds and, again, the plants will readily seed themselves.

A final possibility is to use old York stone flags as a base. This is the most expensive and permanent solution. In this case, I advise you to create formal paths and certainly do not even think of crazy paving instead of rectangular stones, whatever the difference in price. Cement them into paths and sitting areas with small gaps for plants such as thyme and pinks. If your garden is really small, the cost will not be too steep; an alternative, cheaper, suggestion is to use old stone roof tiles which are much shallower than flags. These are best found in the Pennines; other flags are generally available from architectural salvage depots.

Plants to Lift the Façade of a House

We own a Georgian flat-fronted house that is set behind a large front lawn in a village street. We fear that the house is boring in appearance and would like to improve its façade as cheaply as possible – perhaps with plants. Do you have any recommendations?

~

First, you should keep your eyes open when you travel locally to see how others have succeeded in improving their house fronts, because these ideas will probably work for you from the point of view of soil or climate. You do not say which way the house faces. However, even if the façade faces north, there are good-looking climbers which may help. *Hydrangea petiolaris* springs to mind. It is a self-clinging deciduous hydrangea that really grows. It has bright green leaves and white, lacy flowers all summer, and its stems are full of character in winter. Another possibility is *Garrya elliptica* which is evergreen and has curious long grey catkins.

You can try carefully chosen varieties of ivy. We like *Hedera helix* Donerailensis which has neat dark leaves and reddish stems. With ivy, keep it trimmed in a neat rectangle, perhaps between the windows, or in a frame around the door.

Whatever direction your house may face, there are lots of choices. We particularly like wisteria, again a fast-grower, which will eventually swathe enormous walls, and provide waterfalls of light mauve flowers with elegant green leaves in early summer. In winter, its grey stems are good value. Be warned, however, that it can grip Georgian iron balconies like a python. Of course, there are lots of roses, and perhaps you should think of old-fashioned ramblers which do not get leggy at the bottom. We are rather keen on *Rosa x odorata* Mutabilis, which has dainty coral leaves and single flowers that turn from apricot to dark pink. This is a well-mannered plant which does not grow too big.

Another trick to improve a boring-looking house is to make sure it has a good backdrop. Try planting a dark hedge, such as yew, around its back areas, or try using large, interesting trees such as purple beeches, red oaks or sweet chestnuts.

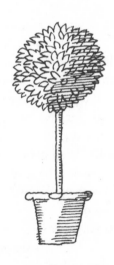

Too Many Trees

I have recently moved to my house in Suffolk and I am trying to tame the overgrown land. The previous owner planted a large assortment of parkland trees between 15 and 20 years ago, which include oak, red oak, walnut, hornbeam, whitebeam, ash, birch, cherry and poplar. By now, it is evident that they have been planted much too close to each other and many will have to be removed. I am very reluctant to cut them down, so can you suggest a viable alternative? I believe that translocation is one option but I have no knowledge of this.

～

You may be onto a winner here as there is a considerable trade in large trees, especially for those who are too impatient to plant saplings and rich enough to take this route. Mature trees are very expensive to buy because you will need to spend a good two years making the roots ready for transplanting (luckily all of your trees appear to be broadleaved and deciduous – conifers are very risky). Mature tree moving has been going on since about 1800, when large trees were moved by horse and cart for noblemen who were keen to have instant parkland, so experts have plenty of background experience as a result. The process requires two years because you will need to dig a trench around half the circumference of the tree, roughly at the limits of its branches and fill the trench with leaf mould. This encourages the roots to become bushy and severs the longer side roots.

The following year, you should complete the process by trenching the other half of the tree and filling this with more leaf mould.

When the root ball is compact and ready in the resting season, you should hire a special machine-cum-trailer that will lift up the tree with a winch. Cover the root ball with sacking and fix the whole tree in the trailer, its roots on the bottom and the trunk in a special slot. This can then be secured and moved wherever you like – it's a good idea to have a hole the size of the root ball already dug, as the less the tree is disturbed at this point, the better. Lower it into the hole and winch the trunk upright. The whole tree will probably need guy ropes to hold it upright for two or more years.

Contractors, such as Nature First (01452 731199) can move younger trees without this preparation.

Restoring Old Cobblestones

Our house, near Oxford, is going on the market. Rather late in the day, it occurs to me that we have rather nice cobblestones in our old stable barn. I wonder if you could tell me where I can find out about the art of laying cobblestones and how common it is to find such floors. When we bought the farm, we covered a lot of the cobbles in the courtyard with gravel to make it more pleasant to walk and drive on. I suspect this was a minor act of vandalism. I should like to pass on any information to my successors.

∿

I have spoken to former ace cobblestone layer, Tony McCormack, who has had to give up the job for his health. He says that if your gravel is just laid over the stones (cobbles are rounded river stones, rather than flat setts), it can be brushed off. If it is tarmacked, the tarmac will peel off and any stains probably vanish in a year. If you used concrete, the news is bad, because the stain can last 12 years.

Laying cobbles is a skill, especially making them look authentic. Mr McCormack says that, in the past, they were laid on a mixture of clay, horse manure and wine. Today, the most common ground is concrete, which 'is not very pleasing'. A lime-based grounding is better, because it will encourage moss and algae between the cracks. You can also lay the concrete short in the joints and fill the difference with a soil mixture. Liquid manure or yoghurt will encourage plants in the cracks.

There are few skilled layers about but, says Mr McCormack, you must find someone with experience, otherwise they will get concrete all over the stones.

Cleaning Panama Hats

How do I clean a panama hat?

I have made extensive enquiries on this. Holland & Holland, which sells them, says to go to a specialist dry cleaner, but neither Jeeves of Belgravia or the specialist laundry Blossom and Browne's will touch them – although Jeeves says they occasionally hand-clean top hats (if that is your next question) and, rather lowering the tone, baseball caps.

So I talked to hatter Herbert Johnson, and the answer is that you can't clean your panama hat because it's too delicate and the stiffening would suffer. You could give it a light sponge-down with water and no detergent, but even that might make it too brittle. The answer, they add, is to buy a new hat or to resign yourself to wearing 'a hat of character'.

Ideas for Monochrome Planting

I know it's a bit late for this year, but thoughts of spring on its way have made me think about planting bulbs for next year. Can you suggest anything startling or unusual?

～

I have just come across a photograph in the current issue of *The National Trust Magazine* of planting at the National Trust's Stourhead. A whole host of tulips is grown in longish grass there (you may need to renew them every year as tulips can be temperamental in grass), but what is really unusual is the black-and-white planting scheme. We've had plenty of white gardens since Vita Sackville-West was at Sissinghurst and black plants are fashionable. But this monochrome mixture is one that I have not seen before.

The tulips are Queen of the Night and Maureen growing at random, probably one-third black and the rest white. It looks extremely elegant. For a closer look, go to Stourhead yourself (check when tulips are doing their stuff on 01747 841152).

The secret, say the gardeners, is to balance the fertiliser carefully – too much will just encourage the grass. Come to think of it, the black-and-white monochrome look could be pushed further into the season – black and white bearded irises, black bamboo beside silver birch trunks and bulls' blood dark beetroot leaves beside the white stems of chard.

Plants for a Warmer Climate

I am about to start to plant a new garden in Lincoln-shire. With the threat of global warming looming, what plants should I choose?

〰

Look towards the sunny Mediterranean, where plants have to cope with long, hot, dry summers and winters which can get frosty and cold. These plants are good at thriving despite fierce drying winds and salt, as you might get on the coast. Many are also evergreen, so that, even in winter, Mediterranean gardens seem to be active all year round. Among those which should cope, even if global warming turns to be slower or less dramatic than expected, are holm oaks, hardy eucalyptus, box and Italian cypress and, of course, herbs such as lavender, rosemary and sage. Many can be clipped into topiary shapes – even holm oaks. There are palms, too, which are resilient, as are figs, acanthus and ivies.

A good start is to get a catalogue from Architectural Plants of Nuthurst, Sussex (01403 891772). Full of these trees and shrubs, it also has a red/yellow/green code, to show exactly how hardy each plant will be.

Importing Italian Plants

*I am going on holiday to Italy this spring and would like
to bring some plants back. What do you suggest?*

～

There are all sorts of regulations about taking plants
between countries (potatoes are particularly dangerous, being classed with firearms and explosives). So you
should read up about the restrictions on moving plants and
also about the possiblity of having a bureaucrat make a
follow-up visit a few months later.

Having said that, seeds are easy: no regulations, no
problems about keeping them alive, no extra weight. In
fact, foreign seeds make excellent presents. If you are in
Italy, virtually every market has a stall full of the sort of
seeds grown by locals – artichokes, lettuce, herbs, rocket
and zucchini – and these will be good and cheap.

Live plants, if you bring those you are allowed (cuttings
are probably safe) should be firmly packed with wadded-up
newpaper wetted under the tap and kept in a sponge bag or
dustbin liner. We once had to buy an entire new suitcase to
bring back about a thousand chive plants given by an
organic farm in Ireland, and they are doing well.

Ideas for Christmas Wrapping Paper

I am so fed up with spending a vast fortune on Christmas wrapping paper only to see it ripped apart without a glance. What is the alternative?

~

I do so agree. Present wrappers have the choice of paying out vast sums (£2 for a small sheet is not unusual) for good-looking gift-wrapping paper or somewhat less for the kind of pap offered by the supermarkets and newsagents' chains. You know, the stuff printed with assorted sprigs of holly, pert robins, ghoulish reindeer and, my personal hatred, rows of portly Father Christmases legging it through the snow.

My solution for attractive, memorable – and cheap – wrapping paper is to think laterally. My first choice, which is easiest for those in big cities, is to wrap presents in foreign newspapers. I especially like Chinese ones which, even if they cannot be read, look both exotic and exciting. Failing that, ones in other alphabets, such as Greek and Cyrillic, are good. My third choice would be anything European, which might be fun to translate over the festive pudding. Failing all these, the *Financial Times* shares page is acceptable. Wrap the present in several layers of newspaper or, for a change, some nice tissue paper underneath (see my next answer opposite for a good source) If the newspaper is black and white, I would go for a red ribbon stuck down with proper scarlet sealing wax (the seal should be covered in Vaseline for a clean job); if the paper is a pink 'un, then the ribbon should be black with either red or silver sealing wax.

All of these look perfectly festive, as well as unusual, and you will have no qualms when the family rips your presents open and the dog then makes papier mâché out of the bits. If, however, you cannot stand such a cheap and sensible option, then any branch of Paperchase has a good selection of elegant plain papers which can be mixed together for a bit of fun. At the extreme top end, I would look out for their beautiful, hand-marbled papers which should only wrap presents for highly civilised aesthetes who know quality when they see it. Such paper should be saved for the bookbinder.

Because I am such an organised person, I like to do my Christmas shopping well before the herd. I also like to organise all the wrapping paper in plenty of time so I can experiment with ideas. This year I am searching for several colours of tissue paper to use instead of boring holly patterns and Father Christmases running in formation. I also want high-quality tissue paper to wrap my cashmere scarves and sweaters and for packing when I travel. Where can I get it?

～

Good tissue paper is very hard to find even in good shops (although most of them use it for wrapping up what you buy). The answer is to grit your teeth and buy it wholesale. Holman & Williams (Packaging) Ltd have a wide range of 44 colours, form Williamsburg Blue to French Vanilla, and they will send you a swatch of them all. You will, however, need to buy a ream of each colour you choose, and this runs to 500 sheets. A ream (how nice that we are still dealing in old-fashioned quantities rather than Euro speak) will cost £30 plus £8 packaging, but if you buy three reams, postage is free. Rob Mattock, the sales manager, says that it is surprising how much you will get through once you have it in stock, and I know he is right.

One clever idea, which I have seen used by fashion firms such as Toast, is to mix the different colours in layers, which gives a much more subtle colour range, and a suggestion of a shot of silk. Toast uses pure white on top with a soft yellow underneath. I like the idea of using black, grey and white for my minimalist friends and, for those of a maximalist tendency, orange and mandarin or dark cerise and burgundy. I suggest that you telephone and ask for a swatch, then play about with colour combinations before ordering two or three reams. Your presents – and your cashmere packaging – will never look better. And, for old prints, silver and so on, the tissue paper is acid-free and colour-fast.

Holman & Williams, Riverside Road, Wimbledon, London, SW17 0BB (020 8879 1100)

Displaying Christmas Cards

Can you advise on how to display Christmas cards?

୰

First, don't hang them up on lines like old washing, even though there are special Christmassy clothes pegs highly priced in the shops. Don't parade them on every surface, because you will need the surfaces for real life and besides, they will all blow over every time you open a door. I have taken advice from two true stylists.

One suggestion is that you push the non-illustrated flap of the card between books in your library (of course, you do have a library) leaving the pretty bit on view. If you have lots of cards, then grade them by size, small ones among the small books and big among the big. This comes from Rosie Inge who, as Prime Minister Gladstone's great-great-granddaughter, knows all about libraries. My second advisor suggests piling them on a large tray to encourage people to shuffle through them, like a photo album. Remember, he adds, to put cards sent by any visitors tactfully near the top.

Decorations

Now my children are grown up, I'd like my Christmas decorations to grow up, too. Can you help?

～

Y ou are right not to get too tasteful if your children are still young – Christmas is really for them. But now they have, hopefully, fled, I think you should get smart by controlling the colour scheme and the amount of glitter, paper chains, tinsel and busy lights. First, ignore those magazines that suggest you cover every mantelpiece, banister and rail with desperately complex wreaths that take a full week to make – life is too short for decorative dementia.

Instead, use natural greenery, such as ivy, holly and fir, to create one large classical festoon in the 17th-century manner and, remember, always overscale. The artist and illustrator Francine Raymond loves playing with natural objects such as dried leaves, twigs and skeletal flower heads to produce soft brown and beige decorations. 'I much prefer them to evergreens as Christmas decorations,' she says. With floristry wire frames, you can make them yourself or buy them at her Christmas shopping event in Suffolk (01359 268322). She also gives courses on decorations and food as presents.

Lucinda Waterhouse, a designer with a special interest in flowers, likes to combine foliage with strong winter colours. 'Vibrant colours are surprisingly easy to find, deep crimson and plum add luxury and style to decorations,' she says. 'Crab apples, mixed with dark amaryllis or branches with red berries, create a festive mood without being over the top. But keep these deep colours to a minimum, just a splash of red will have more impact when used sparingly.'

The Table

How can I make my Christmas dinner table look elegant without breaking the bank?

Simple – keep it simple! We like plain white crockery of absolute purity of design (Asda has a set of 12 bowls and plates for £5.75). A plain platinum band is also acceptable. We like our glasses to be plain, uncut glass in Classical shapes. We like cutlery to be Georgian silver (not as dear as you might think) and the knives to be old-fashioned 'ivory'-handled ones. Mats should be bland and the centre-piece should be an array of plain, beeswax candles of different heights and thickness. Put them in silver candelabra if possible, otherwise plain glass is good. The Headland Hotel in Newquay, Cornwall, props up candles with chunky stones found on the beach. All the colour will thus come from the food and wine, which makes it look especially appetising. Look at Nigel Slater's *The Kitchen Diaries* (Fourth Estate, £25) to see the effectiveness of the minimal approach.

Christmas Lights

I'd like to have some special lights to make my house seem more festive. I want something which is beautiful rather than showy.

Lighting, according to designer George Carter, is the most inventive area in decor today. 'Every year, people have to think up startling styles,' he says. 'White pea lights, of the net variety, are especially useful inside and out – but not flashing – draped over plants and the tree.' We have spotted a snow flake Glow Light at Pedlars (01330 850400, approx. £7.95 each). This is 8cm in diameter and is battery operated. A group is quite beautiful. Hang them over a window or mantlepiece. It's always best to concentrate your effect in groups than scatter about.

Scents

I read that supermarkets waft the scent of freshly-baked bread around their aisles to get people in the mood for buying. What scent should I waft around my house to get people in the mood for Christmas (one to drown the smell of burnt toast, perhaps)?

෮

Winter is a fine time to perfume your house, because you are probably trying to keep the outdoors firmly where it should be. Winter rooms should look inward to glowing fires and polished furniture. Sue Jones, a director of smart design firm OKA, has been researching scented candles before the company launches its own. She told me: 'Scents are very personal, but there are many distinctive smells that immediately conjure up certain seasons, memories and places. For example, cinnamon, orange, wood smoke and pine needles make most of us think of autumn days and Christmas.' There are scented candles dedicated to Christmas which will last for days rather than hours; you could also make or buy an orange pomander studded with cloves, use wintry pot pourri or even (when no one is looking) spray a spicy aerosol around. I suggest that, if you go the artificial route, you should cheat by having pomanders as decoys.

Over the Top?

I like to keep my Christmas devoted to the religious festival. But as I drive home, I am confronted with six bungalows in a row covered with dancing Santa Clauses, prancing reindeer, exploding Christmas puddings and animated Christmas trees – all in non-stop, multi-coloured flashing lights. Can I ask them politely to tone it down?

❧

Once I would have agreed with you but, recently, a friend told me these displays are 'one of the few present-day expressions of folk art on a big scale'. Does that make it better?

PETS & WILDLIFE

Geese – the Watchdog Alternative

My wife is allergic to dogs but, because we live in a remote farmhouse, we need some sort of watchdog. We cannot afford a full-time security man. What can you recommend?

～

Chinese geese make perfect palace guards (in 365 BC, Roman geese saved the Capitol from a Gaulish attack). They are extremely noisy, and, if they spot an intruder (or someone they have taken a dislike to), they make a terrific honking, both day and night. You will get plenty of warning that there may be uninvited guests on your land. Luckily, you do not seem to have neighbours who could get exasperated by the noise.

Chinese geese are also frightening in the way they approach you, and even aggressive if they feel like it – especially at breeding time. Graham Hicks of Hicks Waterfowl World in Oswestry, who reckons he has the largest selection of domestic waterfowl in Europe, says they are his first choice of night-time bouncers: 'Just as effective and far cheaper than men.'

He sells his geese in up to flocks of 40 in large, risky areas such as distilleries and desolate sites prone to vandalism. The geese deter casual baddies not once, but for good. Unless you are protecting a large area, however, he recommends you start with a pair, a goose and a gander, costing about £65 (or £10 each, if you can cope with them at a fortnight old). Otherwise, run a flock of one gander to five geese.

As a bonus, Chinese geese lay about 50 eggs a year and make good broodies. They are extremely decorative, acrobatic and elegant. The downside is that they make a mess and hate yappy dogs, especially poodles or Chihuahuas, which apparently sound just like foxes. If the geese have the temerity to attack you or your dogs, you can get your own back and eat them.

Hicks Waterfowl World, 07818 036118

The Domestic Waterfowl Club: www.domestic-water-fowl.co.uk

Domestic Ducks and Geese by Fred Hams (Shire Books, £4.50)

Feeding Birds In Winter

Now that winter has arrived, I would like to do my bit to feed the birds in my country garden. I have a bird table outside my drawing-room window, and love to see small birds tucking in. Do you have any suggestions about what to give them?

∽

First, you should ignore the Royal Society for the Protection of Birds' latest marketing wheeze. The RSPB ('For Birds, For People, For Ever' – a more meaningless slogan would be hard to find) has jumped on the celebrity bandwagon by hiring celebrity cake-maker Jane Asher to create a little something for our feathered friends. Who next, Gordon 'Blue Tit' Ramsay? She suggests mixing seeds, nuts, dried fruit and bacon rind into melted beef suet or lard and pouring the whole into a coconut shell or old yoghurt pot (to my mind, not that stylish an item to be hanging outside the drawing room).

I am scathing about this because we have been conducting our own bird feeding experiments which prove that suet is not a bird's food of choice. We bought a hanging larder of different types of bird temptation so they had their own *à la carte* choice. There was a bundle of sunflower seeds and another of shelled peanuts. Between those hung two balls of suet with nuts and seeds, much like the Asher bird-brainwave and, at the bottom, there was a large bundle of unshelled peanuts.

This has been hanging under the bird table for a month and not looking particularly beautiful with its lurid plastic mesh. The birds, virtually all tits, have most liked the sunflower seeds and the shelled peanuts, both of which are almost gone. They have pecked in a desultory way at the suet balls, which are hardly touched, and have totally ignored the unshelled peanuts. So, in future, we will buy loose peanuts and various seeds and put them in a more elegant container. A multi perched steel and clear plastic bird feeder (found in most garden centres) is stylish but needs regular washing. We will also throw some of this mixture onto the ground for the robins, finches and sparrows (and forlornly hope the pigeons are not too greedy). Blackbirds and thrushes love windfall apples, so we leave these where they lie. Our woodpeckers have, on occasion, tucked in to the bird table itself.

Ferrets as Pets

My two grandsons, aged 11 and 13, say they want a ferret for Christmas. They live in an old country rectory with outhouses and a walled garden. Before I take the plunge, can you tell me if I will be committing a hideous error, for which my daughter-in-law will never forgive me?

～

Well, that rather depends on your daughter-in-law, but many people do get endless pleasure from their ferrets. Don't think of them in the same way as rats, but rather as otters. Ferrets, like weasels, polecats – from whom ferrets are probably descended – and stoats (as well as mink) are all from the *Mustelidae* family. In the wild, they hunt small mammals – rabbits mostly – and that is what they will do for you. Adrian Dangar, my ferret expert, says the best way to keep a ferret amused is to let it do what comes naturally by taking it rabbiting in winter. But ferrets are also playful: you can exercise them on a lawn (your walled garden sounds good – obviously if you took them into a wood, you might never see them again). Give them romping games (Mr Dangar's played with his dog, but you should take this carefully, in case one kills the other.) It's a good idea to exercise them just before a meal, so the ferret will follow you back into the house. Ferrets are partial to a bit of roadkill, such as squashed pheasant, and Mr Dangar also suggests rabbit livers in milk. Otherwise, they like bread and milk but, sooner or later, they need meat. There are websites which sell cages and accessories, but these often say more about the owners' needs. *The Independent* recently suggested it was a good idea to buy your ferret a hammock (£2.99 at www.petplanet.co.uk) and dress it up as the Phantom of the Opera (£6.99 at www.ferretworld. co.uk) or in a waxed jacket (Burberry are apparently taking action against *Ferret World* for selling 'confusingly similar' clothes). Anyone foolhardy enough to try to dress a wild animal with sharp teeth in a black cape lined with satin deserves to have it run up their trousers. As Mr Dangar says: 'it's all commonsense, really'.

Wasps – An Alternative View

Do you have any suggestions to stop us being annoyed by wasps? Each summer, our pool is besieged by them. We have tried glass 'wasp-jars' containing honey or syrup, but they are ignored.

❧

I am afraid I am not going to be helpful here. People should not want to trap creatures into dying in sticky goo, nor can I advocate killing a whole colony of thousands just because the wasps are annoying around the pool. In *Bees, Wasps, Ants and Allied Insects* (1932), Edward Step says the adjective 'waspish' is a gross libel of the insects. Unlike bees, wasps 'are much more disposed to ignore the big human being, unless the latter is one of the fussy, interfering sort that imagines the rest of creation exists for the purpose of causing him annoyance and loss. He may "swat" the blowfly with impunity… when he tries similar tactics with an armed creature, it is only to be expected that there will be reprisals'. Left alone, wasps will treat unthreatening humans as invisible. Change your frame of mind and remember that, as wasps feed their larvae with insects and grubs, they do good in the garden. So my advice is ignore the wasps, and use good sense in not leaving jam sandwiches lying about by the pool.

Getting Rid of Spiders

I want to use the attic in my thatched house as a proper room, but the spiders have got there first. How can I get rid of them?

⌒

This is difficult as thatch and spiders are a natural duo. A spider expert tells me that spiders don't like the atmosphere to be hot and dry, and suggests that you put in double glazing and turn the heating up. This, to my mind, is worse than actually having spiders. Another suggestion, made quite firmly by someone who has coped with the problem, is to put conkers wherever you can in the room. Spiders do not like anything to do with chestnuts. I heard the same story from a guide at one of the great châteaux of the Loire. When I asked if the beams, 20ft or more above, were hard to rid of cobwebs, I was told the beams were made of chestnut wood (sweet chestnut, in this case) and the spiders automatically kept their distance. As now is the time to pick up conkers, why not try this method first?

Dog Hairs

My large, short-haired dog insists on getting into bed with me, which creates problems when I go to stay in holiday cottages. Can you advise me how to cope?

～

It would be too much, I imagine, to make the dog keep out of your bed when you stay away. If so, the answer is to take your own sheets when you visit places.

Strip off the cottage sheets, especially the bottom one, and use your own (if there's a duvet, insert your top sheet under it). Your dog is, I hope, unlikely to mess up anything than the sheets.If the same goes for chairs and sofas in the cottage, take a large rug with you and drape it over the dog's chair. These precautions ensure that your dog does no damage.

You would, however, be surprised at the way people leave holiday cottages (and hotel rooms, no doubt). They don't wash up after breakfast, they stain chair covers with indelible ink, break the crockery and leave, taking the keys with them.

One hotel owner I know says he'd much rather have dogs as guests, because they don't smoke in the rooms and never kiss the chambermaids (except in the nicest possible way).

PARTIES

Portable Loos

We are having an event in our grounds and expect lots of people to turn up. Obviously, they will need lavatories throughout the afternoon – can you tell me how many I should hire?

~

You do not tell me exactly what event you will have and this has some bearing on the matter. For instance, if you are opening your garden or having an exhibition in an outbuilding, although you might expect 500 people in a day, none of them will stay very long (a maximum of two hours, I should think) and their arrival and departure will be staggered. Also, they will probably neither eat nor drink that much. In that case, your visitors will be unlikely to need many lavatories.

But if you are planning a wedding or some other party, then you can expect all the guests to arrive – and leave – more or less together. Also, they will be eating and drinking over a period of several hours, especially in the case of weddings which, these days, can last 10 hours or more. And guests will be wearing their best clothes.

If this is what you are planning, you will need to be liberal with lavatories to make sure that long queues do not develop. It can be very embarrassing for party guests, especially women, to queue in the rain outside a portable loo in their best clothes and hats.

To find out more, I talked to Glenis Noton of Classical Toilet Hire of Bury St Edmunds (01359 253556). They hire mobile lavatories of the utmost grandeur – 'gold' taps, dried flower arrangements and the like – which would put most of our own bathrooms to shame. These are named after English authors with the Shakespeare the biggest and the Brontë the smallest (the Huxley is for staff and puts old Aldous in his place).

Mrs Noton says they work on one loo per 50 guests. For a large party of between 350 and 400, they would recommend three ladies', two gents' and three gents' urinals; for 200 guests, you would need two ladies', one gents' and two urinals and for 100 – a pretty normal number – only one ladies' and one gents'.

Fund-Raising Auctions

I am trying to raise money for our parish church in a medium-sized village. I have heard that other villages have organised 'slave' auctions and wonder if you can tell me anything about how they work and whether they are likely to make money for us. Can you advise the best way to organise such an auction?

'Slave' auctions put together those with skills and those who need to employ such skills – all for the benefit of charity. The 'slave' offers an hour or so of expert time and the buyer agrees to pay rather more than this is worth to help that charity. Your medium-sized village is, therefore, better than a small one because you will need to get enough 'slaves' to offer their services free, and eager buyers to spend at auction more than they would in the real world. You will also need a place – the village hall; a barn? Plenty of local notices to get buyers to turn up and some printed catalogues listing the lots on offer (these could be sold for about £2 as an entry fee).

Patricia Hodgkins, who has run such auctions, has made more than £4,000 for a parish church. She told me that not only does the event raise money and help those who need work done, but 'I like it as a method of mixing people as much as anything. Real friendships have been formed as a result – one "lot", help in tracing family history, has developed into regular trips to record offices round the country for a couple of new friends.' Mrs Hodgkins finds her 'slaves' through careful research. 'I go round the village asking everyone about their hobbies.'

The auction is crucial. First, ply your bidders with a glass of wine (included in the ticket price) then offer even more wine at £1 a glass to loosen the wallets and the atmosphere. Ensure that the auctioneers have the right mix of jollity and bullying. In Mrs Hodgkins's village, the auctioneers used various ridiculous props such as wigs, stuffed toys and banjos.

'If you can't get a real auctioneer, I recommend barristers or amateur actors,' she says. Two other people, accountants for example, should guard the cash box, ensure everyone pays up quickly and gives each successful bidder a promissory note. Christie's and Sotheby's might learn a thing or two.

Catering for a Wedding

I have been let down by the hotel which was to cater for my wedding party of 20. I have found a charming new venue. However, there are no catering facilities there – although we have been offered the use of an outhouse which has plenty of electric sockets – and all the local caterers are booked up. What can I do?

༄

Look in your local paper for a cheap electric cooker which you should be able to buy for less than £100. Plug this in in an outhouse and use it for heating some ready-made food. You can make this yourself in advance or find a local deli/restaurant which will do it for you the day before. You can even, at a pinch, get this from the supermarket (Waitrose is particularly helpful).

Try something such as soup with good bread and butter, followed by, say, coq au vin or braised lamb shanks with baked potatoes and then a cold pudding. You should be able to heat up the first two courses, one after the other, in your new cooker and warm any plates on a plate warmer or in hot water in a sink. After the party, re-advertise the cooker at the same price.

An alternative is large-size thermos flasks as used for shooting parties, but they are expensive if you only use them once.

Wedding Cake Equipment

When our daughter gets married in October, I have decided to make the wedding cake myself. Can you let me know where I can find all the equipment?

〜

Well, that's brave of you (and parsimonious as well). Your best bet is to go to Cake Creation of Wallasey (0151 639 0192), where they sell (or hire) every conceivable object connected with cakes. The firm will sell you all the ingredients needed for fruit cakes – or you can buy ready-made ones in descending sizes, as well as marzipan, dried fruit, ready-made sugar flowers and all other sorts of decorations you might want – or the equipment to make them with. They sell nozzles and smoothers for the icing as well as display stands for your cake, and even the little boxes to send cake slices to those who couldn't attend. The only snag is that this is a small firm which does not do regular mail order; but, if you ask them nicely and pay the postage, all should be well. Failing that, many bakeries which make wedding cakes will hire out their equipment for a one-off cake-making session. I wish you, your daughter and her fiancé the very best of luck.

Tea Ceremony Dilemma

A group of Japanese visitors has asked to come and visit my garden and to be given tea later. I am not sure I am up to creating a tea ceremony. I can get sencha green tea and, probably, handleless cups, but is this enough? And what should I give them to eat?

~

Do not worry. A friend of ours was faced with exactly this dilemma and she bought all the necessary green teas, tiny cups and so on, just as you propose. Then she had the good idea of asking the tour guide and interpreter what she should serve. The surprising answer was Yorkshire tea, just as a builder likes it, with English sandwiches. Actually, if you think about it, how would you feel if, on going to have tea in a Japanese garden, they gave you Yorkshire tea with cupcakes and scones? Not best pleased is my guess.

Before I even read your answer to 'Tea Ceremony Dilemma' in Country Life, *my eyes were drawn to the photograph of teacups. Could you possibly send me some information on them? I do hope you can help me.*

~

They were lovely cups, and they came from Fortnum & Mason (020 7734 8040) in London. Sadly, they were about £25 each – but probably worth it for the pleasure of taking tea every day.

Seating Plans

*We are planning a lunch party to celebrate our parents'
40th wedding anniversary, inviting about 70 people. My
sister says we need a seating plan, but it seems to me that
this would spoil the informal atmosphere we want to
create.*

～

If by informal, you mean chaotic, with crowds of guests
vainly trying to find a place to sit – away from bores or
enemies who they don't want to talk to (no gathering this
size is without hidden agendas) – go ahead. Even a party of
10 needs a seating plan.

Anyone who has ever been a guest at an unplanned party
will know the embarrassment and annoyance this can
cause. You are left at a table and no one comes to join you;
there are only three places left at a table for 10; you end up
next to the person you've been talking to for half an hour
and are trying to avoid. Seating plans are essential. I cannot
say this strongly enough.

To avoid over-formality, however, mix your guests up –
young and old, married and single, guests from different
families. Try to put people beside like-minded others, do a
bit of networking with an important businessman next to
a lad looking for a career, a hotel owner beside a would-be
chef. I know it takes time to organise (have a slip of paper
for each guest and larger bits of paper for each table), but,
believe me, it is fun. You will have a much better party as a
result.

Which Tea Cups?

Every year I organise at least one tea party in the village and wonder if you have any views about what crockery to use?

～

Pure white is all the rage, but I do not think that village tea parties should be chic. My choice would be good old willow pattern. It's traditional, it's charming and the blue and white design is just right for villages.

More to the point, virtually every pottery makes willow pattern, so you will be able both to get plenty of rejects and to replace broken cups and saucers with new. Whatever you may feel about it, willow pattern is unlikely ever to be discontinued.

FOOD & DRINK

Meat Safes

*I have a small cottage in the country where it is imposs-
ible to fit in a large fridge (and my small one is always
looking full). So I am looking for a traditional meat safe
which I could keep in the cellar. I would use it to store food
which does not need to be kept very cold but should be away
from mice and flies. Do you know where I can get one?*

All my enquiries with the traditional kitchen suppliers,
ironmongers and even catering firms have drawn a
blank, other than a useless small cheese-keeper only 10in
high. Indeed, the lads at some firms had never heard of
them. The best answer is to look round in kitchen antique
shops (where they will not be cheap), car-boot sales,
country auctions or even, if you want one with a grand
pedigree, country-house sales.

Meat safes, with three of their sides simply covered in
a fine mesh, were once standard, and there are still quite a
few about. They were used exactly as you intend. There is
always a point when food is warm and should not be put in
the fridge. There are also foods which like to be kept at
room temperature, but away from flies.

If, however, you are not keen on car-boot sales or auctions, a meat safe is fairly easy to make (or, more likely, get
made by a handyman), or you can adapt a fitted cupboard
in a cool part of the kitchen, by replacing the solid door
with a screen.

At least ironmongers still sell perforated zinc, which is

perfect for the job and easy to attach with small nails. The zinc costs about £3.86 a square foot (traditional iron-mongers have not yet gone metric and quite right, too).

Meat Safes (revisited)

When I last wrote about meat safes, I admitted failure in the buying department. I had tried all the usual suspects – the kitchen shops, the mail-order equipment firms, even old ironmongers. What I did not do was to try the upmarket mail-order storage companies. But here, at last, is a source.

The excellent Holding Company, started by an American Dawna Walter to try to put some method into British organisational madness, has a splendid selection in its catalogue, available now. There is a zinc cabinet which combines a shelved cupboard with mesh doors below with another, open, shelf above which is extremely stylish indeed, being all-over metallic (£170). If the mesh is a bit too open to stop flies easing their way in, you can back it with a fine, light muslin.

Then there is a series of wire-fronted cupboards: the bedside cupboard is extremely narrow and has a pull-out drawer above a cupboard with a wire door (£130 in zinc), the Holloway cabinet has two wire-fronted doors and no extra shelves above and costs £170 in zinc. Two further cupboards are 156cm tall. The single-door doctor's cupboard is exactly what it says – the same height with double doors (£315, zinc). Both have five shelves and should be big enough for nearly all your meat-safe needs, even at Christmas.

As the catalogue points out, these cupboards can be used for many other tasks – in the bathroom, the bedroom and the office – because the zinc is also transparent you can see what is where at a glance. Many of the cabinets have optional legs so, if you want them on a shelf rather than the floor, they will sit quite firmly. The Holding Company also has a series of fabric wardrobes, starting at £68, which can be adapted to keep food away from flies (although mice might be able to eat their way in). Each has a metal frame on which to stretch a fine fabric cover which zips up. You need to assemble these but, of course, they can be taken away when not needed.

The Holding Company is on 020 8445 2888;
www.theholdingcompany.co.uk

Baking Scones

At the ripe old age of 56, I have decided to learn how to bake scones. It is difficult even to find recipes for these as they are so unfashionable, and I cannot understand what some of the ingredients are. Can you tell me about the following: baking powder, bicarbonate of soda, tartaric acid, cream of tartar, arrowroot, cornflour and ground rice? And, while I'm at it, what are pectin and agar-agar?

⌐

Let's start with the simple ones: cornflour is flour made of ground-up maize (sweetcorn), and ground rice is, obviously, rice ground up. Either is good mixed with plain flour for scones. Baking powder is a raising agent (not a leavening one, like yeast, which ferments, if we are going to be pedantic), and it is made of cream of tartar, bicarbonate of soda and salt. Alternatively, you can use either cream of tartar (which is the same as tartaric acid and comes from grape juice after the grapes are fermented for wine making) or bicarb of soda (baking soda, sodium bicarbonate) on their own, preferably with sour milk (which, by the way, is almost impossible to find).

Follow a recipe by an experienced scone maker – WI cookery books have some good ones, as do those hand-written notebooks from the 1950s you might find in second-hand bookshops. Scones and other varieties of British baking are, as you say, unfashionable, and you will search a long time through today's chic cookbooks to find anything helpful.

But you should be able to buy these ingredients at the supermarket. Arrowroot is a flour made from tropical roots and called after the Native American word for flour-root – araruta. It is used for thickening sauces, rather than in baking, and, like cornflour, is less likely to go lumpy than ordinary flour. Agar-agar, an Eastern seaweed, and pectin, a carbohydrate extracted from fruits, are aids in getting jams and jellies to set. Unlike the more common gelatin, made from bones and tendons, these are both vegetarian. While I am at it, self-raising flour has baking powder already added; plain flour does not.

What to Do
With Leftover Gazpacho

In the recent hot spell, I learnt to make gazpacho, iced and deliciously cool, for lunch. Invariably there is some left over. Any suggestions?

∽

Copy the Spaniards, is my suggestion, and turn the liquid into a sauce rather than a soup. Seafood is particularly good here: a handful of tiny shrimps, some flaked cooked haddock or crab (one of my pet hates but a common addition). You could also put in scraps of fried bacon or chippings of ham, add peeled chopped tomatoes and cucumber, black olives and peppers. While we are on the subject, a good tomato soup can be reworked as a sauce for pasta with chopped tomatoes, sweated onions and garlic added, and clear onion soup with extra onions makes a good gravy with sausage and mash.

Making Kedgeree

We have recently moved into an old farmhouse and my parents are coming to stay for a weekend. I want to give them kedgeree for breakfast. Can you give me a simple recipe?

⤳

We always use Elizabeth David's quick version, which never lets us down. For four people, you chop and fry a medium onion into 2tbs of olive oil until cooked, but not browned. Add curry powder to your taste (she suggests a teaspoon, but I would use more like a tablespoon) and a handful of sultanas. Then add four heaped tbs of rice and swirl the whole in the oil. Take a large fillet of undyed smoked haddock, pour boiling water over and leave for at least three minutes, then remove the skin and any bones, and flake into pieces. Hard-boil two or three eggs, and chop them into small bits when cool. All this can be done in advance. To finish the dish, add a pint of boiling water to the rice mixture and cook steadily, but not at a gallop, for 10 minutes, stirring occasionally with a fork. Add the haddock and cook until the rice is done – probably 10 minutes. Check whether you need salt – the haddock may contribute enough. Then scatter the eggs and chopped parsley on top, and serve with plenty of mango chutney, half a lemon each and, for the greedy, a dollop of butter.

Sausage Roll Recipes

I would like to try making my own sausage rolls rather than buying them from the baker. Despite having dozens of recipe books, I have been unable to find any mention of them at all.

～

Sausage rolls are extremely unfashionable, which is strange, because sausages are having a revival. To make them is simple: buy sausage meat from your local butcher, or buy fancy sausages and remove the skins to make your own sausage meat. Then either buy or make some rolled puff pastry. Roll out the sausage meat to pieces 2½in long with a 1½in diameter, and wrap the puff pastry around it, closing the long end with egg wash. Wash egg over the top of the pastry and cook in a hot oven (200°C/400°F/ Gas 6) until the pastry is a rich golden colour – about 15 to 20 minutes.

You might like to add your own spices and flavours to the sausage meat: fried onions chopped very fine, a hint of curry powder, a touch of tomato ketchup or Tabasco sauce, or some fresh thyme or sage. Sausage rolls are delicious served with boiled broccoli or cabbage, and they are good for picnics, too.

Falling Cakes

I keep having failures with my baking. I have tried to cook a chocolate cake three times and, each time, it has been uncooked in the centre and, when I try to take it out of the cake tin, the centre flops out and it looks like a Polo mint.

There are two possible problems here. The first is that you may be using a dud recipe. Despite what home cooks believe, not every recipe is tried and tested. I would suggest you try a different recipe from a different book: Delia Smith is said to be foolproof.

The other problem may be that your oven is not doing what you think it is. Our Aga, despite the gauge saying it is under-heating, is, in fact, hotter than it makes out. Your oven may be less hot than you think. I would buy an oven thermometer – good value at about £6 – and just check before you cook anything that is temperature sensitive.

Beef Leftovers

I love roast beef, and always buy a really large joint – 6lb on the bone is normal. Of course, we never eat it all in one sitting. What can I do with the leftovers?

Rare roast beef is delicious cold, served with mustard or horseradish sauce, butter and the best bread you can find. You probably already know this. Otherwise, here is a Swedish recipe (for four) that we all love. For 1lb of cold beef you should have five peeled potatoes, ½lb streaky bacon, two onions, four fresh eggs, chopped parsley, butter, olive oil and seasoning.

Cut the potatoes, onions, bacon and beef into tiny dice. Heat butter and oil in a large pan, add the potatoes and cook for 15 minutes until golden brown. Remove and keep warm. Add onions, beef and bacon to the frying pan and cook for 10 minutes, stirring constantly, until all are cooked. Add the potatoes and fry for 10 minutes more until all are crisp and inviting. Season and mix in the parsley. Arrange in piles on four plates, make a hole in each centre and drop in a raw egg (or a fried egg if this worries you). Serve mixed well with Worcestershire sauce and Tabasco, like steak tartare. Delicious, and in Sweden it's served with pickled beetroot.

A reader replies:

I have one more suggestion for leftover beef. Really rare, cold roast beef is delicious with good traditional mayonnaise (i.e. handmade). Add good French bread or even chips, and you have a feast.

Other Ideas for Leftover Food

Although there seem to be hundreds of cookery books published every year for every known cuisine, I can find nothing about what to do with leftovers. I know this is not a glamorous subject, and that the likes of Gordon Ramsay and Jamie Oliver don't even have to think about cold chicken and mince, but we do. Do you have any suggestions?

I do so agree, but perhaps any cook under 50 just throws out the leftovers or gives them to the dog (sometimes, even the dog misses out). Those who grew up with economical habits find this disregard for leftovers not only absurd but uneconomic (and, surely, not very Green). One cookery writer who does address the issue is Nigel Slater, but he tends only to use the good bits.

My best suggestion is to find a copy of Marika Hanbury-Tenison's book, *Left Over for Tomorrow*, which was published by Penguin in 1971 for a derisory 50p (those were the days). You can now buy it secondhand via Amazon at a less agreeable £45. But it will still save you the money in no time, as well as suggesting all sorts of delicious dishes. Why Penguin doesn't reissue this defeats me – but I suppose it is irredeemably unglamorous. No good for name-dropping and celebrities. You can't imagine Victoria Beckham cooking leftovers – or, indeed, anything at all.

Homemade Lemonade

In this continuing heatwave, I would love to enjoy a huge jugful of delicious homemade lemonade. Do you have a recipe for this quintessential summer drink?

~

You will need ½ pint water, 4oz sugar and three lemons. Pare the rind off the lemons as thinly as you can. Put the rind and the sugar into a pan with the water already boiling. Stir until the sugar is dissolved. Let it stand until cool, then add the freshly squeezed juice from the lemons. Stir and strain it and put it in the fridge until nice and cool. Dilute it down with chilled water to your taste.

Incidentally, *A Little Book of Recipes for Cooking with Herbs* (published by M. G. Scott, Blo' Norton Hall, Diss, Norfolk) suggests adding chopped leaves of lemon balm and borage to the mix when you remove the pan from the heat. Then, when you make the drink, add the borage flowers and some salad burnett.

Any cold drink, even tap water, will get extra marks if you add fresh herbs. Mint is a good one, as are balm, verbena and borage or a slice of lemon or lime and a few borage or lavender flowers.

Making Mint Tea

I am just back from Marrakech where glasses of mint tea were wonderfully refreshing in the heat. Now that I am back and it is hotter in London than the Sahara, can you tell me how to make it?

～

You will need green tea (2tbs to ¼ gallon of water) plus a good handful of fresh spearmint (or any fresh mint) and 125g of sugar cubes.

Boil a kettle. Put the tea into a nice silver teapot (the Moroccans use a style similar to the Queen Anne period) and pour on a little water. Swill it round and pour off to remove any dust and the tea's natural bitterness. Add the torn-up mint and sugar and pour over the rest of the water. Leave for 6 to 7 minutes. Pour the mint tea from a height, to oxygenate it, into proper Moroccan mint-tea glasses.

Drying Walnuts

I have a number of walnut trees and each year a large amount of nuts go to waste. Can you make any suggestions as to how I can dry them to stop them going mouldy, especially as I have heard that the mould is carcinogenic?

〜

I n his encyclopedia *On Food and Cooking*, Harold McGee recommends that fresh walnuts should be dried with as little heat as possible: 90–100°F/32–38°C. They should then be stored in opaque containers in a cool place. Alternatively, when they are fresh and green, they are delicious in salads, with cheese or fresh grapes. Or you could try to sell them via a farm shop – ours does.

British walnuts usually lack sun – therefore, are short of oil and tend to shrivel when dried. They can, however, be preserved in a moist, fresh state (without drying) for four to five months, in the following way:

Take a plastic dustbin with a well-fitting lid. Collect the nuts and allow all the green husk to fall off. Make a mixture of equal volumes of table salt and fine sawdust from a joiner's shop. As you collect the nuts, lay them in the dustbin, cover each layer lightly with the salt/sawdust mixture. Keep the lid on the dustbin at all times to prevent the salt from attracting atmospheric moisture.

The nuts may be eaten at any time and develop a delicious taste, far better than ordinary dried nuts. To eat, brush off the salt/sawdust and crack in the normal way. I have used this method here for the past 45 years, having learnt it from my grandfather. The nuts eventually become strong tasting, but can remain good until the next Easter.

A reader writes:

Walnuts fall when they are ripe. Collect them. Remove the husks, freeing the shells of any fibrous material, using a scrubbing brush, but NO water. Dry at room temperature. Store them in a large jar or earthenware crock, alternating layers of nuts with layers of equal quantities of salt and sawdust. I remember doing this with the large crops in 1942 or 1943, and they were delicious at Christmas.

Storing Coffee Beans

How should I store coffee? I'm told it's best kept in the freezer.

～

Y ou can store coffee beans in the freezer, but not for longer than a month, after which the oil in the beans may start to spoil. The best solution for all coffee, beans or ground, is to buy it vacuum-packed, or in tins. When you open it up, it's slightly better to keep it in the fridge or a cold larder than in the warm. Better still is to buy your coffee in small quantities. Opened packs of beans will last about two weeks, and ground coffee only a week, when stored in a cold place.

Keeping Salt Dry

We live on the west coast of Scotland and, among other problems, our salt keeps going damp and rock-like. What can I do?

～

I would follow the Italians in this. Whenever you go to a trattoria, you will find that the salt shakers have about

20% of rice grains mixed with the salt. They take up the moisture from the salt, leaving the crystals dry. When you buy salt in boxes, I would suggest that you decant it into a glass jar, and mix it with rice for the same result.

Removing Avocado Stones

I have a friend who was badly injured when trying to remove an avocado pip with a knife. The knife slanted off the stone, easily penetrating the pear's flesh and her hand. How should pips be removed?

Avocadoes should have a health warning attached. So many injuries are caused by trying to ease out the large stone with a sharp knife. Never use one. If the pear is ripe, just squeeze it until the pip is loosened, and then ease it out by hand. Otherwise, scoop it out with a dessert spoon. This may not look as neat as the knife version, but it doesn't cripple you for life.

Life for Liqueurs

I have been given a bottle of plum liqueur and another of raspberry. Other than drinking them neat, can you suggest ways of using them? They look so tasty, but I'm not a liqueur person myself.

∽

Well, the first thing is to use them instead of cassis in kir, or kir royale (the fizzy version). Both are just as good as cassis, but interestingly different. For something less alcoholic, you could treat them as you do cordials and add to sparkling water in the same way you would elder-flower cordial. Or, here's another idea, make a spritzer with them. Mix a small measure of liqueur with a mixture of half-and-half white wine and sparkling mineral water and serve on a hot day with a slice of lemon and ice.

Then again, you can add them to foods, if that does not seem a bit of a waste. We think they are delicious on ice creams or sorbets – raspberry on raspberry sorbet and plum on plum or plain vanilla. They make a very good addition to cold baked fruit, too, and, in the case of raspberries, the liqueur could be poured over fresh fruit instead of cream. In Italy, they pour white wine, still or sparkling, over rasp-berries and strawberries.

Gin Cocktails

Can you sort out the difference between the following gin cocktails: Gin Pahit, Gin Sling, Gin Rickey, Gin Fizz, and Tom or Gin Collins? I keep coming across the names in books by authors such as Somerset Maugham and would just like to know what the characters are drinking.

⌇

Here are the answers: Gin Pahit is a Pink Gin – neat gin with a few drops of Angostura bitters.

A Gin Sling is made of gin, lemon juice and sugar syrup, stirred together and topped with fizzy water or soda.

Gin Rickey is the same, but lime juice replaces the lemon.

Gin Fizz is more confusing. At its simplest, it is gin shaken with ice and sugar syrup and strained into a glass with ice cubes and topped with soda or fizzy water. This is also a Tom or Gin Collins – except that the Collins is put in a larger glass. A Golden Fizz has an egg yolk added and a Silver Fizz has the egg white. Royal Gin Fizz has the whole egg. Ramos Gin Fizz, notoriously difficult to make, was invented in the late 19th century in New Orleans. It consists of gin, lemon and lime juice, cream, egg white, soda, powdered sugar and orange flower water.

Personally, I'd stick to a good old gin and tonic.

Whisky Sours

I loved finding out about gin slings, which reminded me that F. Scott Fitzgerald would write about his characters drinking whisky sours. What are they? They always sounded so thrillingly grown-up.

〜

These great cocktails bring back Hemingway and Chandler and Humphrey Bogart and Edward G. Robinson, who looked like a menacing hippo. A whisky sour is whisky shaken with lemon juice, a bit of sugar and crushed ice, which is strained off, served on the rocks or straight up, sometimes with a maraschino cherry and an orange slice. You can also do the same with bourbon, gin and rum.

DECORATIVE
ARTS &
ANTIQUES

GLUE

Labelling Antique Porcelain

Over the years, I have accumulated a large collection of Chinese objects. Most are pieces of 18th century export porcelain painted with European crests, but there are also red lacquer pieces, and some small stone carvings such as Chinese chop seals. I would like to attach to each my collector's mark and details of each individual item. How do I go about this?

❧

Many collectors have special stickers printed for their objects and these are often seen in the auction houses where such identification can attract premium prices, as well as helping less knowledgeable buyers.

Those I have seen in this house and elsewhere have always been circular with, in the centre, the monogram or crest of the collector involved. Information about the specific article is generally inked around the edge. Such information might simply be a catalogue number which refers back to a written catalogue, or more likely today, a computer disc.

Alternatively, you can add basic details in this space with your crested porcelain, for example, the name of the crest's original owner or family. Today, you can have your small circles printed with a self-adhesive backing. It is equally possible to find labels that are licked. In either case, make sure the bond will not damage any surface. There should be no problem with either porcelain or polished stone, but it may be a good idea to ask a conservator about lacquer or anything else you are worried about.

Your local printer will quote you a price for the circles, with your collector's mark in the centre (Ink in Print of Bury St Edmunds has quoted me £51 for 200 and £60 for 500, plus VAT, in the unlikely event I have the artwork on disc). You will also need a mapping pen and black Indian ink for the tiny writing needed round the edge.

Hallmarks Explained

I recently saw an article in a national newspaper about silver hallmarks, which was illustrated with a mark that included the initials EPNS. I have some old spoons with just such a mark. Can you tell me what it means?

～

I'm afraid that the photograph in the article was wrong. EPNS stands for Electroplated Nickel Silver. It is not silver but silver plate and, as such, will eventually wear down to the base metal with use.

With the exception of jewellery, all British silver has been required by law since the Middle Ages to carry a hallmark. Although this has varied over the years, each piece of English silver will have a date letter, a town mark and a walking lion or a leopard's head, which may be crowned. Each of these denotes silver of sterling quality. If the head is 'erased' (looking as if it has been pulled off) and comes with the figure of Britannia, the silver is of a higher purity (or is intended for export). Instead of the lion, Edinburgh silver has a thistle, and Dublin silver has a crowned harp. Outside London, English towns with their own hallmarks include York, Newcastle, Sheffield and Exeter.

If the hallmark is clearly punched, then the quality, date of manufacture and origin of a piece of silver can be easily determined. Hallmarks can sometimes identify the manufacturer. Most silver dealers will happily sell small volumes deciphering the hallmarks, enabling you to do your own detective work.

Cleaning Silver

Ten years ago, we were given a harlequin set of 19th-century silver Old English spoons and forks as a wedding present and, since then, they have sat under our bed wrapped in felt. We have decided this is silly and intend to use them. Can you tell me how to clean the tarnish and how to keep them in good order?

⌇

I am glad to hear they have been kept in felt and that you are going to use them. Silver that has been wrapped in newspaper can be seriously spoilt by the acid in the printing ink; similarly, elastic bands can stain silver in a few days. Make sure all your silver is in felt, fabric bags or acid-free tissue paper.

Your decade-old tarnish will take some shifting. Silvo liquid should be applied and rubbed on with a soft duster and thereafter polished up with another soft duster. If the pieces are still not good enough, keep putting on Silvo and polishing until you are satisfied. Ornate patterns (unlike Old English) which cannot be reached with Silvo can be cleaned with Goddard's Silver Dip and an old toothbrush – but it is essential not to leave silver in the dip too long. Follow the maker's instructions meticulously. When the silver comes out of the dip, give it another polish with Silvo before washing in hot soapy water to get the surplus polish off.

Once your pieces are gleaming, it is easy to keep them in good order. Your main problem will be ignoramuses who offer to wash up and proceed to clean the spoon bowls with a scourer. This will undo years of building up a soft patina and result in visible scratches which create a matt effect. One silver dealer advises that in this emergency – and only in emergency – the silver should be given a single polish with tougher Brasso. In general, however, you should maintain the flatware with regular use of Goddard's Silver Foam, a soft pink amalgam of jewellers' rouge (the silver dealer's polish of choice). This can be done during normal washing up and will even remove those nasty black stains on the egg spoons.

You will love using your Old English silver – one of my favourites – and miss it when you travel from home. It is both robust and not too valuable. I would advise getting expert advice on grander pieces.

Cleaning Silver Gilt

I would be most grateful if you would let me know how I should clean two Victorian silver gilt bonbon dishes. I have asked jewellers and antique shops but nobody seems to know. Thanks for an interesting column.

～

The Goldsmiths' Company has given me this advice: silver gilt is quite difficult to clean and antique pieces are best done through a professional silversmith.

However, you can do quite a good job by giving them a clean in soapy water (such as Fairy Liquid) and then a quick dip in Goddard's Silver Dip (using a fresh solution), but do not leave them in for more than a few seconds. Then rinse and rub off with a soft cloth. Creams and cleaners can be too abrasive for silver gilt.

The Goldsmiths' Company also warned that it is not a good idea to put hollow-filled items in a dip (i.e. candlesticks, which might be filled with plaster of Paris or pitch) as the solution could start to erode the filling. Silver Dip is only good for cutlery, bowls and so on (like your bonbon dish, I imagine); also, don't put anything in that has another material involved, such as wood, or a hairbrush with bristle. As extra care should be taken with these, it's probably safest to use a silver polishing cloth – both the Goddard's and Town Talk ranges include one.

With modern pieces (this does not include Victorian), it's fairly straightforward to have them re-gilded. If the piece is antique, it gets a bit more problematic as it may actually detract from the value, so do check with an expert first. Re-gilding will cost about £2 per square inch, but most silversmiths would probably charge a minimum fee of about £60 to £70.

Cleaning Old Pewter

I have just discovered a box full of pewter in my attic, where it has been since it went out of fashion in the 1940s. I am told some pieces are good 18th century antiques. All are dingy and dirty. How do I clean them up?

～

Humourless purists would shudder at the mere idea of cleaning up antique pewter, especially if it has 'scale' – those flaky black marks. Scale is a sign of age and therefore, in collectors' minds, importance. I take the opposite view, for who wants dingy tankards all over the shelves? Pewter should shine with that typically steely glint and, I am glad to say, the Pewterers' Company naturally agrees with me.

Charles Hull, the curator of the company's collection and a restorer himself, firmly told me that, just as we clean antique silver of tarnish, we should also clean pewter. 'My feeling is that it should be treated like silver and, at the company, we are getting it back to how it would have looked originally.' But, the question is, how to do so.

Mr Hull says it all depends on the oxidisation or tarnish. New pewter is easy, and simply needs a wash with silver foam about once a year – pewter tarnishes far more slowly than silver. If your antique pieces are just dirty with little tarnish, then a brass polish should bring them back – Brasso or Duraglit are the brands.

Finally, faced with really bad tarnish, Mr Hull resorts to a dip in a mild caustic soda solution. 'I put about two handfuls of caustic soda into a bucket of water and put the piece of pewter in for about 24 hours.' This is not quite as simple as it sounds – wear rubber gloves and add the soda to the water not vice versa (it might explode). Then rinse the piece well. 'The problem is that the oxide is harder than the metal and you may find cleaning it off makes holes. But at least the caustic does not attack the metal. Collectors also use wet and dry sandpaper.'

If the piece is important or valuable, go to a restorer like Mr Hull (01225 334716) who will have buffing tools and can patch up holes – although even that is difficult as the pewter alloy (tin and lead) can vary in colour.

If you need to know more, Mr Hull recommends the Shire Album 280, *Pewter*, which is out of print but may be found second hand.

Labelling Portraits

There is much debate in our family about some 19th-century portraits we own. Some of us would like to commission those small gold labels (like you see in museums and stately homes) to give details of the sitter and the artist; others would like to add other details such as wife, children and decorations. Yet another faction says the whole thing is pretentious.

~

If your family had seen as many old portraits as we have which are simply called 'Portrait of a Gentleman' or 'Portrait of a Lady', your pretentious faction would be quickly silenced. For the sitter to have lost all identity is a small tragedy. Nor should you imagine that this happens gradually – we have recently seen a charming portrait of a young woman, painted, we would guess, in about 1930, who has already lost her name. So, yes, label your paintings even if the pretentious faction insists these are kept hidden on the back.

Our view about contents on the plaque is that the artist, where known, should be identified with whatever relevant initials he had after his name at the date of his death (for example, RA). The sitter should be given his or her name, date of birth and any title or honours. If the portrait shows an adult sitter, the date of death is also acceptable. In our view, putting these details on a portrait of a child is ludicrous – imagine a pretty little Victorian boy in a sailor's outfit labelled Maj-Gen Sir Cuthbert Fox, KCB 1874– 1932.

Instead, put Cuthbert Fox, aged six, 1880. We also feel that, in some cases, the sitter's occupation or estates should be included such as Mary Wilkinson, author, or Archibald McClaren of Glen Almond. Other details such as 'founder of the Hebburn chemical works' or 'mother of 23 children' are best left off the main plaque and kept, with other details, in an envelope attached to the back of the frame or the canvas stretchers.

Depending on the date and style of the painting, the lettering should be simple serif capitals for the sitter and sans-serif for the details of the artist. We prefer the plaques to be made of wood, gilded with gold leaf, on which the lettering is hand-done in black paint. Brass is unnecessarily ostentatious.

Replacing Lost Cutlery and Crockery

About 20 years ago, we lost a knife from a 12-piece setting canteen. Since then, whenever I am in an antique shop, I have looked to find a matching replacement, but without luck. I have also written to Walker & Hall, the makers, but I think the firm has been taken over by another manufacturer; in any event, they did not seem able to help me.

The canteen contains 12 large and 12 small knives, and it is a small knife that is lost, bone-handled, stainless steel, with tiny brass dowels on the sides of the bone handle. Do you know anyone who replaces lost cutlery?

∽

There are several firms which will search out pieces of crockery to complete broken bits of a whole dinner service, but I fear that there are no similar ones for cutlery – perhaps because it does not break easily and the chances of losing a piece are not that common. This is no help to you, of course. However, Chinasearch, 4 Princes Drive, Kenilworth, Warwickshire CV8 2FD (01926 512402; www.chinasearch.co.uk) have recently started to search in this field.

As a result of your query, Chinasearch's owner, Helen Rush, has added Walker & Hall to the list of makers' names that interest them. She says that if you get in touch, they will put the details of your knife on file and try to find a replacement for you.

At the same time, you might think of going to eBay to see if the internet auction site can help. Who knows, there may be dozens of W&H small knives scattered throughout the world waiting for you. There are certainly nearly 70 Walker & Hall pieces at present listed, although no small knives.

Camden Passage Market (Wednesday and Saturday) in Islington, London, regularly has at least one stall selling a good selection of old cutlery, as does Robson's Antiques in Barnard Castle (01833 690157).

However – and I know this is not what you want and that the missing knife probably reduces the value of your canteen – but if you can search the antique shops for a small knife which is virtually the same in all details but the maker, surely it will suffice around the table? Most guests, thankfully, do not compare the small knives at a party.

∽

I recently read your article on missing pieces of cutlery. Another possible source here in the United States is www.replacements.com, which does list a few pieces/patterns of Walker & Hall flatware. Perhaps this may help other readers who have the same problem in finding missing pieces. Replacements also handles crystal, china, collectibles, etc.

Painted Floors

We have just bought our first house, spending up to the hilt. We cannot afford any form of carpet, whether fitted or otherwise. We have some rugs, but the wooden floors are painted a nasty brown around the edges where previous unfitted carpets have not reached. Please help.

～

Your answer is to use a good floor paint (Farrow & Ball's are the ones we used) and paint the entire floor area unless you want the rather more expensive option of sanding out the dark painted bits and then covering the whole with a matt varnish. However, painted floors are very much the mode and, if you pick an off-white such as F&B's Pointing or Hardwick White, the room will be measurably lighter when you have finished – although, of course, it will need mopping from time to time. A dark paint such as Down Pipe, a near black, is highly dramatic and good if you have plenty of light and space already. White furniture looks wonderful on it. You can paint the stairs as well to avoid the expense of a stair carpet. If your rugs are large enough to sit before the fireplace, assuming you have one, then pick a floor paint to complement the rug.

Enamel Initials on an Antique Watch

An uncle has recently left me his watch because his name, Iain Harrison, is the same as mine. More to the point, the watch is made of gold and from the Edwardian period. It has his name, 12 letters long, enamelled on the face instead of the usual numerals. The problem is that whoever created that face (clearly not a Scotsman) thought Iain was a collection of initials and the watch reads I.A.I.N. HARRISON. I would like to get the full stops removed. Is this possible?

～

Sorry, Mr Harrison, I would not recommend going down that route. Enamel is made of powdered glass which, at high heat, is fused into a continuous surface. You can no more scratch out bits of it with impunity than you could a pane of glass. I have spoken to various jewellers who say scratching might succeed in removing the full stops, but the copper surface below would be revealed and would leave a nasty mark of its own. Any other kind of intervention could easily result in the enamel surface cracking permanently. Best leave well alone and change your name to Iain Andrew Ivor Norman, or some such suitable collection. Or, better yet, just stop worrying about it.

Restoring Cast-Iron Baths

I hope you can help me. I have a very large, old, luxurious cast-iron bath, more than 6ft in length, which is looking very tired and worn, but I just do not want to throw it away. Apart from anything else, it would be an absolute nightmare to get the old thing out of my house.

I seem to remember an article in the magazine about a company that can restore my old bath in situ, hopefully back to its former glory. Is this correct? If so, please inform me, and others like me, of this company.

∽

The firm is Renubath (see also page 27) and it will come to your house to restore your old cast-iron bath (and I do agree that you must keep it – modern baths are not the same). Renubath is on 0800 138 2202.

Flying the Flag

My husband wants to fly a flag of his own design from a turret of our Victorian house. I thought I would buy one for his birthday. How do I go about it?

❧

Your husband obviously realises that any respectable country house should have a flagpole; and any respectable flagpole should have a flag. Having your own flag made to order is relatively easy and not outrageously expensive. First, decide on the design. It is unthinkable that a flag should be illustrated with words or monograms or pictures. It must be geometric.

Our household has a flag which displays its rather chic coat of arms; in heraldic speak 'Argent a chevron between three fleurs de lys Gules on a chief embattled Sable three mullets Or' with, entirely surrounding it, a red and white chequered border which denotes the third son. We had hoped to avoid this last because, when hand sewn, as the best flags are, hundreds of small appliquéd red squares tend to be expensive and it was a Christmas present. But, no, the heraldic expert insisted.

Flags today are no longer of whip-cracking heavy cotton canvas but of spun polyester which, actually, is a good thing. It fades more slowly and it lasts longer. Our household's is coloured black, gold and scarlet – good eye-catching stuff. We consulted carefully with the House of Flags, which make flags to order, and they showed us a selection of varied golds and scarlets before we went ahead. The design was 'mirror imaged' so it looks identical from each side and then the whole came ready to fly, with ropes and toggles.

We ordered it at 1.2m by 1.8m – the size of a single bed-spread. Never, ever, have too small a flag – they look really stupid. You must always order them bigger than you think possible – do a test with a curtain or blanket. The House of Flags in Kimbolton (01480 861678) told me that, today, our flag would cost roughly £222.

Applying for a Coat of Arms

How do I go about getting a coat of arms?

✌

You will need to 'petition' the Earl Marshal at London's College of Arms (020 7248 2762), who will only grant arms if you can 'demonstrate some input into society', and if you are a subject of The Queen. Therefore, if you live in Surbiton or Sydney, Nassau or Nantwich, you are eligible – except if you are Scottish or Canadian, in which case you should petition the Lord Lyon King of Arms in Edinburgh (0131 556 7255) or the Chief Herald of Canada in Ottawa.

Once you have passed this mild vetting, you will be invited to call at the College of Arms to discuss the devices and colours to be used on your coat of arms. The final decision is made by the College, which insists that the arms are tasteful and conform to the rules of heraldry. The same goes for the motto, which can be in any language from Chinese to Hindi, although English, French and Latin are the most common.

When the arms are agreed, they will be drawn by an expert heraldic artist on calf-skin, 18in by 24in, and signed and sealed by the Kings of Arms – Garter, Clarenceux or Norroy. The total cost is £3,800, although it will be more if you have supporters (usually for peers) or something fancier.

Glass Repairs

We have a pair of Murano glass geese (about 15in long, quite heavy) given to us as a wedding present in 1959. They're old but treasured. One of them has a broken beak, about an inch long, which is stuck on badly and held with Sellotape. It needs an expert glass repairer. Do you have any ideas where it might be possible to get this done?

～

Glass repairs can be done, but by experts (the Roman Portland vase was rebroken and repaired by the British Museum a few years ago). Your best bet would be the London firm of Wilkinson, based in Catford Hill, London se6 (020 8314 1080). The firm, which has been going for generations, has a Royal Warrant. If London is too far, I recommend that you ask your local museum if they know any glass conservators. They might have someone on the staff who can do it, or they may know a freelancer.

Reframing a Portrait

When clearing out a relative's house, I discovered a charming picture of my great-grandmother as a young girl. The trouble is that the oil painting has been cut down by an anonymous vandal so there is virtually nothing left but her head. What can I do to rescue the situation?

⌇

The secret here is to get it framed well. Pretend to yourself that this is not a mutilated full-length picture for which someone should be mutilated themselves, but is a small painting of a girl's head by, say, Degas or Renoir. If it were, it would have an extremely grand frame of the period, with touches of gilt and plenty of moulding. It might also have a canvas or gilt slip. You will find that, treated like this, it will at once look something special.

If you do not know a good framer (and one is essential) you might try John Jones (020 7281 5439) in London, who not only have a huge selection but will happily advise. If you should visit, you will be amazed at the paintings they are working on for the best London galleries, which is an excellent recommendation. Not cheap, but worth every penny.

Engraving a Salver

My parents have handed down to me a salver that they were given as a wedding present in 1929. It is of exceedingly good quality, but they never got round to engraving the family coat of arms on it as they had intended (which I think is a pity). Would it be right to do this now and how should I best go about it?

In theory, I suppose, to put a later coat of arms on a salver might be considered a bit naughty, but I hardly think you would be reducing the value of the salver, especially if the family coat of arms might have actually been put on at this date.

Many top jewellery firms would be able to organise etching a coat of arms for you, but one I would recommend is the Hatton Garden firm of Andrew R. Ullman of 36, Greville Street, EC1 (020 7405 1877; enquiries@arullman.com) to do this for you. The price should be about £300.

Index